OHIO

Travel Guide 2025

Discover the Heartland's Hidden Gems and Must-see Destinations

Sarah H Lokken

Ohio Travel Guide 2025

ALL RIGHTS RESERVED.

No part of this publication may be reproduced, distributed, or transmitted in any form or by any means, including photocopying, recording, or other electronic or mechanical methods, without the prior written permission of the publisher, except in the case of brief quotations embodied in critical reviews and certain other noncommercial uses permitted by copyright law.

DISCLAIMER

This travel guide is provided for informational purposes only. The information contained herein is believed to be accurate and reliable as of the publication date, but may be subject to change. We are not making any warranty, express or implied, with respect to the content of this guide.

Users of this guide are responsible for verifying information independently and consulting appropriate authorities and resources prior to travel. We are not liable for any loss or damage caused by the reliance on information contained in this guide.

Information regarding travel advisories, visas, health, safety, and other important considerations can change rapidly. Users are advised to check for the most up-to-date information from official government and travel industry sources before embarking on any trip.

Travel inherently involves risk, and users are responsible for making their own informed decisions and accepting any associated risks.

Ohio Travel Guide 2025

ABOUT THE AUTHOR

Sarah H. Lokken is a passionate traveler and acclaimed travel guide writer who has journeyed through over 40 countries. With a knack for uncovering hidden gems and a deep appreciation for diverse cultures, Sarah's guides are beloved by both seasoned globetrotters and first-time adventurers. Her writing is infused with vivid storytelling and practical insights, making her books both a delightful read and an invaluable resource.

Sarah's love for exploration began in her childhood, where family road trips sparked a curiosity for the world beyond her doorstep. She later pursued a degree in Cultural Anthropology, which further fueled her desire to connect with people from different backgrounds and understand their ways of life.

When she's not exploring new destinations, Sarah enjoys sharing her travel experiences through travel guides. She is dedicated to inspiring others to embark on their own adventures and to embrace the transformative power of travel.

Ohio Travel Guide 2025

TABLE OF CONTENTS

INTRODUCTION..10
    Welcome to Ohio... 10
    How to Use This Guide... 11
    Ohio at a Glance... 14

CHAPTER 1: PLANNING YOUR TRIP......................17
    Best Times to Visit Ohio..17
    Essential Travel Tips... 19
    Packing Checklist... 22

CHAPTER 2: GETTING TO KNOW OHIO...................26
    Ohio's Geography and Climate...............................26
    Quick Facts About Ohio..28
    History and Culture of Ohio.................................... 30

CHAPTER 3: TOP DESTINATIONS............................ 34
    Columbus: The Capital City.................................... 34
    Cleveland: On the Shores of Lake Erie................... 37
    Cincinnati: The Queen City.....................................40
    Dayton: The Birthplace of Aviation......................... 44
    Toledo: The Glass City...47

CHAPTER 4: OUTDOOR ADVENTURES................... 52
    Hiking at Hocking Hills State Park.......................... 52
    Kayaking on Lake Erie..55
    Rock Climbing at John Bryan State Park...............58
    Zip Lining at Mohican State Park........................... 62

CHAPTER 5: SCENIC ROUTES AND ROAD TRIPS..66
    Ohio River Scenic Byway....................................... 66
    Amish Country Byways...69

Lake Erie Coastal Trail..72
Great Miami Riverway... 76

CHAPTER 6: CULTURAL AND HISTORICAL ATTRACTIONS.. 80
Rock & Roll Hall of Fame..80
National Museum of the US Air Force.................... 84
Stan Hywet Hall & Gardens...................................... 88
Wright Brothers National Memorial..........................93

CHAPTER 7: FAMILY FRIENDLY ACTIVITIES........... 98
Family Fun at the Columbus Zoo and Aquarium.... 98
Rocking Out at the Rock and Roll Hall of Fame... 102
Thrills and Spills at Cedar Point Amusement Park..... 105
Hands-on Learning at the Imagination Station..... 109
Adventures at Kings Island Amusement Park.......113

CHAPTER 8: DINING AND CUISINE......................... 118
Must-Try Ohio Foods... 118
Best Restaurants in Ohio..120
Food Festivals and Events..................................... 123
Farmers' Markets...125

CHAPTER 9: ACCOMMODATIONS...........................128
Luxury Hotels...128
Mid-Range Hotels... 131
Budget-Friendly Options... 135
Unique Stays... 139

CHAPTER 10: TRANSPORTATION AND GETTING AROUND...144
Public Transportation Options................................144
Car Rentals and Ridesharing................................146

Ohio Travel Guide 2025

- Bike Shares and Scooters 150
- Navigating Ohio 153

CHAPTER 11: LOCAL FESTIVALS AND EVENTS .. 158
- Annual Festivals Calendar 158
- Seasonal Events 161
- Special Cultural Celebrations 164

CHAPTER 12: SAMPLE ITINERARIES 171
- Weekend Getaway in Columbus 171
- One-Week Road Trip Through Ohio 174
- Family Vacation Itinerary 180
- Adventure Seeker's Guide 186

CHAPTER 13: DAY TRIPS AND NEARBY ATTRACTIONS 192
- Ohio's Amish Country 192
- Geneva-on-the-Lake 195
- Ohio State Reformatory in Mansfield 198
- Serpent Mound Historical Site 202

CHAPTER 14: TRAVEL RESOURCES 206
- Comprehensive List of Emergency Contacts 206
- Traveler Resources and Websites 209
- Budgeting and Cost Estimation 213

FREQUENTLY ASKED QUESTIONS (FAQs) 218
- Why Visit Ohio? 218
- Getting Current Road Conditions 220
- Ohio State Parks Information 223
- Upcoming Fairs and Festivals 226

BONUS SECTION: LOCAL RECIPES TO TRY AT HOME 229
- Ohio Buckeye Candies 229

Ohio Travel Guide 2025

Cincinnati Chili... 232
APPENDICES... 236
    Glossary of Local Terms... 236
    Useful Maps and Directions.................................240
CONCLUSION..253
    Final Travel Tips... 253
    Inspirational Quotes...256
    Thank you note.. 259

Ohio Travel Guide 2025

HOW TO SCAN

1. Open your phone's camera.
2. Point it at the QR code.
3. Wait for it to focus.
4. Once recognized, tap the notification.
5. Follow the link or information provided.

OHIO

Ohio Travel Guide 2025

INTRODUCTION

Welcome to Ohio

Ohio is a state filled with delightful surprises, from bustling cities to serene countryside. Here's a brief guide to get you started:

In Columbus, start your journey in the state capital. Explore the Scioto Mile for stunning riverfront views and visit the vibrant Short North Arts District with its eclectic mix of galleries, boutiques, and eateries. The North Market is a must for fresh produce and global delicacies.

Next, head to Cleveland. Don't miss the Rock and Roll Hall of Fame. After soaking in music history, head to the West Side Market for some local food, especially the delicious pierogies!

For nature lovers, Hocking Hills State Park is a paradise with stunning landscapes, including Old Man's Cave and Ash Cave. Perfect for hiking and photography, it's a place to reconnect with nature.

In Cincinnati, the Cincinnati Zoo & Botanical Garden is great for a family outing. The Over-the-Rhine district is known for its historic 19th-century buildings and lively brewery scene. Make sure to visit Findlay Market for local treats.

When it comes to local flavors, in Dayton, you'll find a delightful culinary scene. Try Ohio's signature dish, Cincinnati chili, at Skyline Chili or Gold Star Chili.

Ohio's festivals are another highlight. The Ohio Renaissance Festival is a memorable event with period costumes and jousting tournaments. For a modern vibe, ComFest in Columbus celebrates community and arts with live music and food trucks.

Ohio's rich history, cultural diversity, and natural beauty make it a perfect destination. Whether you're exploring urban centers or seeking out quiet retreats, Ohio has something for everyone.

How to Use This Guide

This travel guide is intended to help you make the most of your vacation to Ohio, whether you're a first-time tourist or a seasoned visitor. Here's how to go through the guide:

Explore by City
Each portion of the book is organized into key cities and areas, including Columbus, Cleveland, Cincinnati, Dayton, and Hocking Hills State Park. This structure enables you to readily access information relevant to each area. Start with the city you wish to visit first and work your way through the others.

Key Attractions and Highlights
Within each city segment, you'll discover a list of must-see sights and highlights. These are the top sites and activities that you shouldn't miss during your vacation. Use this as a checklist to arrange your trip.

Local Flavors
Discover the various food and drink experiences Ohio has to offer. This section highlights the distinctive meals and local places you should try. It's a terrific opportunity to immerse oneself in the local culture and tastes.

Outdoor Adventures
Ohio is home to lovely parks and natural scenery. The book offers suggestions for outdoor activities, such as hiking, photographic sites, and picturesque vistas. Perfect for people wishing to discover nature.

Cultural Experiences

From museums and historical sites to arts districts and festivals, this area includes cultural events around Ohio. It gives insights into the local artistic scene and historical relevance, boosting your trip experience.

Insider Tips
Throughout the book, you'll uncover insider advice and personal stories that will help you travel like a native. These ideas include optimal times to visit, hidden jewels, and guidance on navigating the cities.

Safety and Practical Information
For a comfortable trip experience, the book gives practical advice on safety, transit, and lodging. These recommendations are essential for organizing your vacation and ensuring a good stay.

Seasonal Events
Ohio has a number of festivals and events throughout the year. Check the brochure for information on seasonal events that could overlap with your visit. These events may offer a particular flavor to your trip experience.

Customizable Itineraries
Based on your interests and time available, utilize the recommendations to construct your own unique plan. Whether you're traveling for a weekend or an extended stay, you may adapt your arrangements to fit your tastes.

By following this guide, you'll be well-prepared to see Ohio's numerous attractions and have a wonderful travel experience.

Ohio at a Glance

Ohio, the Buckeye State, is a blend of vibrant cities, charming small towns, and breathtaking natural landscapes. Located in the heart of the Midwest, it offers a unique mix of cultural, historical, and recreational attractions that cater to all types of travelers.

Major Cities
- Columbus: The state capital, known for its dynamic arts scene, innovative culinary offerings, and the bustling Short North Arts District.
- Cleveland: Home to the Rock and Roll Hall of Fame and a thriving cultural scene, including theaters, museums, and a renowned food market.

- Cincinnati: Famous for its historic Over-the-Rhine district, beautiful riverfront, and the Cincinnati Zoo & Botanical Garden.

Natural Attractions
- Hocking Hills State Park: A nature lover's paradise with picturesque trails, waterfalls, and caves. It's perfect for hiking, camping, and photography.
- Lake Erie: Offering beautiful beaches, fishing, boating, and the scenic Lake Erie Islands.

Historical Sites
- Dayton: Known for its aviation history, including the National Museum of the United States Air Force.
- Marietta: Ohio's first settlement, rich in historical landmarks and museums.

Food and Drink
- Savor local specialties like Cincinnati chili, pierogies in Cleveland, and the burgeoning craft beer scene across the state.
- Visit food markets like North Market in Columbus and Findlay Market in Cincinnati for a taste of local produce and artisanal goods.

Cultural Experiences
- Enjoy the diverse arts scene, including performances at the Ohio Theatre in Columbus,

Playhouse Square in Cleveland, and the Cincinnati Music Hall.
- Participate in annual events like the Ohio Renaissance Festival and ComFest in Columbus, celebrating arts, music, and community spirit.

Insider Tips
- Visit during the fall for beautiful foliage and festivals.
- Explore beyond the major cities to discover charming small towns and scenic countryside.

Ohio's blend of urban excitement and natural beauty makes it a destination with something for everyone. Whether you're an adventure seeker, history buff, or foodie, Ohio promises a memorable travel experience.

CHAPTER 1: PLANNING YOUR TRIP

Best Times to Visit Ohio

Ohio is a year-round destination, each season offering its own unique charm. However, some times of the year are particularly ideal for experiencing the best the state has to offer.

Spring (March to May):
Spring in Ohio is a delightful time as the state comes alive with blooming flowers and mild temperatures. It's perfect for outdoor activities like hiking in Hocking Hills State Park or strolling through botanical gardens. The Cleveland International Film Festival, held in April, is a highlight for movie enthusiasts.

Summer (June to August):
Summer is a popular time to visit Ohio, especially for family vacations. The weather is warm and ideal for enjoying Lake Erie's beaches, water sports, and the

vibrant festivals across the state. The Ohio State Fair in Columbus is a must-visit, offering everything from carnival rides to concerts and agricultural exhibits. Cincinnati's Riverfest and Cleveland's outdoor concerts also make summer an exciting time to explore.

Fall (September to November):
Fall is arguably the best time to visit Ohio. The state's foliage transforms into a stunning array of reds, oranges, and yellows, making it perfect for scenic drives and outdoor activities. Oktoberfests in cities like Cincinnati and Columbus offer a taste of German culture with food, beer, and music. Hocking Hills State Park is especially beautiful this time of year, with its breathtaking fall colors.

Winter (December to February):
Winter in Ohio brings a magical, festive atmosphere. The colder months are ideal for enjoying holiday events and winter sports. The Christmas lights at Clifton Mill and the holiday markets in Columbus and Cleveland are enchanting. Skiing and snowboarding in places like Mad River Mountain and Snow Trails add to the winter fun.

Overall Recommendations:
- Best for Outdoor Activities: Spring and fall offer the most pleasant weather for hiking, sightseeing, and exploring nature.
- Best for Festivals and Events: Summer and fall host numerous festivals, fairs, and outdoor concerts that showcase Ohio's vibrant culture.

- Best for Budget Travelers: Winter, outside of the holiday season, can be less crowded and more affordable for accommodations and attractions.

Each season brings its own unique experiences, so depending on your interests, there's always a good time to visit Ohio.

Essential Travel Tips

When planning your trip to Ohio, keeping a few essential travel tips in mind can help ensure a smooth and enjoyable experience. Here are some key tips to consider:

Weather Preparedness
Ohio's weather can be quite variable, so it's important to dress in layers and be prepared for changing conditions. Check the weather forecast before your trip and pack accordingly. In winter, make sure to bring warm clothing, and in summer, light, breathable fabrics are best.

Transportation
If you're planning to explore multiple cities, renting a car is a convenient option. Ohio's public transportation options vary by city. Columbus has a decent bus system, while Cleveland's RTA offers buses and light rail. For shorter trips within cities, ride-sharing services like Uber and Lyft are widely available.

Local Cuisine

Make sure to try some of Ohio's local specialties. Cincinnati chili, Buckeyes (chocolate and peanut butter treats), and pierogies in Cleveland are must-tries. Visit local markets like the North Market in Columbus and Findlay Market in Cincinnati for fresh, local produce and unique food items.

Safety Tips

Ohio is generally safe for travelers, but it's always good to stay aware of your surroundings, especially in urban areas. Keep your belongings secure, and avoid walking alone in unfamiliar areas at night.

Accommodation

From luxury hotels to budget-friendly options, Ohio has a wide range of accommodations to suit every traveler. Book your stay in advance, especially during peak travel seasons or major events, to ensure the best options.

Health and Wellness

Stay hydrated, especially if you're visiting during the warmer months. If you have any specific health needs, make sure to carry necessary medications and a first-aid kit. It's also a good idea to have travel insurance.

Cultural Etiquette

Ohioans are generally friendly and welcoming. When visiting rural areas or smaller towns, a polite greeting and showing respect for local customs go a long way.

Tipping is customary in restaurants and for services like taxi rides and hotel staff.

Technology and Connectivity
Most urban areas and many rural spots have good mobile network coverage. Wi-Fi is widely available in hotels, restaurants, and cafes. It's useful to have a mobile map app and download offline maps for areas with limited connectivity.

Local Events and Festivals
Check local event calendars before your trip. Ohio hosts a variety of festivals, fairs, and events throughout the year that can add a unique experience to your visit. Planning around these events can also help you avoid crowds or find special activities to enjoy.

Budgeting
Ohio is relatively affordable compared to many other U.S. states. However, costs can add up, especially in major cities and tourist areas. Plan your budget in advance, considering accommodation, transportation, meals, and entrance fees to attractions.

By keeping these essential travel tips in mind, you'll be well-prepared to explore Ohio and enjoy all the amazing experiences it has to offer.

Packing Checklist

Preparing for a trip to Ohio? Here's a handy checklist to ensure you pack everything you need for a comfortable and enjoyable visit:

ESSENTIALS
- Passport
- Keys
- Travel Documents
- Wallet
- Cash, Credit Cards
- Pen
- Book or Magazine
- Snacks
- Gum

ELECTRONICS
- Camera
- Laptop
- iPad or Tablet
- Headphones
- Back up Battery
- Charger

TOILETRIES
- Toothbrush + Toothpaste
- Deodorant
- Hairbrush + Comb
- Razor
- Hair Ties
- Tampons + Pads
- Shampoo + Conditioner
- Makeup + Makeup Remover
- Moisturizer + Serums + Eye Cream
- Hair Products
- Perfume
- Body Wash
- Body Lotion
- Face Mask
- Facial Cleanser
- Sunscreen + After Sun Care
- Lipbalm
- Handcream

CLOTHING
- Underwear
- Bras
- Tops
- Jacket
- Denim
- Dress(es)
- Skirt
- Shorts
- Sneakers
- Sandals
- PJs
- Socks
- Swimwear
- Sweaters
- Flip Flops
- Belt

PERSONAL ITEMS
- Sunglasses
- Glasses or Contacts
- Hat
- Eye Mask
- Scarf
- Neck Pillow
- Jewelry
- Evening Bag

HEALTH
- Aspirin/Ibuprofen
- Vitamins
- Kleenex
- Band aids
- Prescriptions Meds
- Hand Sanitizer
- Nail File
- Insect Repellant
- Pepto-Bismol/Immodium

Clothing
- Layers: Ohio's weather can be unpredictable, so pack layers for varying temperatures.

Ohio Travel Guide 2025

- Comfortable Shoes: Ideal for walking and exploring.
- Rain Gear: A waterproof jacket or umbrella.
- Seasonal Items:
  Spring/Fall: Light sweaters, long-sleeve shirts, and jackets.
  Summer: Lightweight clothing, hats, and sunglasses.
  Winter: Heavy coat, gloves, hats, scarves, and thermal wear.

Toiletries
- Basics: Toothbrush, toothpaste, shampoo, conditioner, and soap.
- Skincare: Sunscreen, moisturizer, lip balm.
  Personal Hygiene: Deodorant, razor, feminine products.
  First Aid Kit: Band-aids, antiseptic, pain relievers, any prescription medications.

Tech Gear
- Chargers: For phone, camera, and other electronic devices.
- Portable Power Bank: To keep your devices charged on the go.
- Camera: For capturing memories, if not using your phone.
- Travel Adapters: If traveling internationally.

Travel Documents

- ID/Passport: Necessary for travel and identification.
- Tickets: Plane, train, or event tickets.
- Itinerary: Copies of hotel reservations, rental car bookings, and other important documents.
- Travel Insurance: Policy details and emergency contact numbers.

Comfort Items
- Travel Pillow: For comfort on long journeys.
- Blanket/Scarf: For warmth during travel.
- Snacks: Non-perishable snacks for the road
- Water Bottle: Reusable and easy to refill.

Entertainment and Guides
- Books or E-Reader: For reading on the go.
- Travel Guides/Maps: Useful for navigating and planning.
- Journal/Pen: For notes and reflections.

Miscellaneous
- Backpack/Day Bag: For daily excursions.
- Reusable Shopping Bag: Handy for purchases and eco-friendly.
- Sunglasses: Essential for sunny days.
- Bug Spray: Especially important for outdoor activities.

Double-check your list before you leave to make sure you haven't forgotten anything. With this packing checklist, you'll be well-prepared to enjoy all that Ohio has to offer.

CHAPTER 2: GETTING TO KNOW OHIO

Ohio's Geography and Climate

Ohio is located in the Midwestern region of the United States, bordered by Pennsylvania to the east, West Virginia and Kentucky to the southeast and south, Indiana to the west, Michigan to the northwest, and Lake Erie to the north. Its diverse geography and climate offer a variety of landscapes and weather patterns.

Geography
- Landforms: Ohio's terrain is generally flat to gently rolling. The state is divided into five geographic regions: the Great Lakes Plains, the Till Plains, the Bluegrass Region, the Appalachian Plateau, and the Lake Erie Shoreline.
- Great Lakes Plains: Found in the northern part of Ohio, this region is characterized by flatlands and rich agricultural soil. It includes the Lake Erie shoreline, which is known for its beaches and recreational areas.
- Till Plains: Covering the central and western parts of the state, this region features rolling hills and fertile farmland, making it a significant agricultural area.
- Bluegrass Region: Located in the southwestern part of Ohio, it is known for its gently rolling hills and fertile soil.

- Appalachian Plateau: This region spans the eastern and southeastern parts of Ohio, characterized by rugged hills, forests, and valleys. It is a mix of highlands and lowlands, providing scenic landscapes.
- Lake Erie Shoreline: The northern border of Ohio along Lake Erie features picturesque views, recreational beaches, and important port cities like Cleveland and Toledo.

Climate

Ohio has a humid continental climate, with four distinct seasons and considerable variations in temperature and precipitation.

- Spring: March through May sees mild to warm temperatures, with blooming flowers and occasional rain showers. It's a beautiful time for outdoor activities and exploring nature.
- Summer: June through August is warm and sometimes hot, with temperatures ranging from 70°F (21°C) to 90°F (32°C). It's the perfect time for beach outings, water sports, and attending festivals.
- Fall: September through November brings cooler temperatures, ranging from 50°F (10°C) to 70°F (21°C). The state's foliage transforms into vibrant colors, making it an ideal time for scenic drives and hiking.
- Winter: December through February can be cold, with temperatures often dropping below freezing. Snowfall is common, especially in the

northern regions near Lake Erie, making it suitable for winter sports and festive activities.

Ohio's diverse geography and climate offer a wide range of experiences, from urban exploration and cultural events to outdoor adventures and serene natural landscapes. Whether you're visiting in the bright summer sun or the crisp fall air, Ohio's geography and climate enhance its rich array of attractions.

Quick Facts About Ohio

Statehood: Ohio became the 17th state of the United States on March 1, 1803.
Capital and Largest City: Columbus is both the state capital and the largest city in Ohio.
Nickname: Known as the "Buckeye State" due to the prevalence of buckeye trees.
Population: Ohio is home to over 11 million residents, making it the seventh most populous state in the U.S.
Geography: Ohio features diverse landscapes, including flat plains, rolling hills, and the Appalachian Plateau.
Major Rivers: The Ohio River, which forms the southern border, and the Cuyahoga River, known for its "burning river" history.
Great Lake: Lake Erie borders Ohio to the north, offering recreational activities and scenic views.
Economy: Ohio has a diverse economy with strong sectors in manufacturing, finance, healthcare, and agriculture.

Education: Home to numerous renowned institutions, including Ohio State University, one of the largest universities in the U.S.

Sports: Ohioans are passionate about sports, with major professional teams like the Cleveland Browns (NFL), Cincinnati Bengals (NFL), Cleveland Cavaliers (NBA), and Cincinnati Reds (MLB).

Inventions: Ohio is known for many inventions, including the Wright brothers' first powered flight in Dayton.

Historical Figures: Birthplace of several U.S. Presidents, including Ulysses S. Grant and William Howard Taft.

Tourist Attractions: Popular destinations include the Rock and Roll Hall of Fame in Cleveland, the Pro Football Hall of Fame in Canton, and Cedar Point amusement park in Sandusky.

State Symbols:
- Bird: Northern Cardinal
- Flower: Scarlet Carnation
- Tree: Ohio Buckeye

These quick facts give you a snapshot of Ohio's rich history, diverse landscape, and vibrant culture. Whether you're planning a visit or just curious about the Buckeye State, there's always something new to discover!

History and Culture of Ohio

Ohio's rich history and vibrant culture are deeply intertwined, offering a fascinating tapestry of stories, traditions, and innovations.

Early History
Ohio's history dates back thousands of years to the ancient mound-building civilizations like the Adena and Hopewell cultures, who constructed impressive earthworks that can still be visited today, such as the Great Serpent Mound. The region was later inhabited by various Native American tribes, including the Shawnee, Delaware, and Miami.

Colonial and Statehood Era
The area now known as Ohio was explored by the French in the 17th century, and later became part of the British

Empire following the French and Indian War. It was incorporated into the Northwest Territory in 178Ohio achieved statehood on March 1, 1803, becoming the 17th state of the United States. The state played a crucial role in the westward expansion and development of the nation.

Industrial Revolution
The 19th century saw Ohio rapidly industrialize, becoming a hub for manufacturing and transportation. The Ohio and Erie Canal, and later the railroads, spurred economic growth and migration. Cities like Cleveland, Cincinnati, and Columbus grew as centers of commerce and industry. Ohio also played a significant role in the abolitionist movement and the Underground Railroad.

Modern Era
In the 20th century, Ohio continued to innovate, contributing to the aviation industry with the Wright brothers' first flight in Dayton. The state became known for its diverse economy, ranging from manufacturing to finance and healthcare. Ohio's cities have since evolved into vibrant cultural centers, each with its unique identity and attractions.

Cultural Highlights
- Music and Arts: Ohio has a rich musical heritage, being home to the Rock and Roll Hall of Fame in Cleveland. The state has produced numerous influential musicians across various genres.

Columbus and Cincinnati boast thriving arts scenes with theaters, galleries, and music venues.
- Festivals: Ohio hosts a wide array of festivals celebrating everything from music and food to local heritage and seasonal events. Notable festivals include the Ohio Renaissance Festival, ComFest in Columbus, and the Cincinnati Music Festival.
- Sports: Ohioans are passionate about their sports, with a strong tradition in both professional and collegiate athletics. Major sports teams include the Cleveland Browns (NFL), Cincinnati Bengals (NFL), Cleveland Cavaliers (NBA), and the Cincinnati Reds (MLB). College football, particularly the Ohio State Buckeyes, is also a major part of the state's culture.

Historic Sites
- National Museum of the United States Air Force: Located in Dayton, this museum showcases the history of aviation and space exploration.
- Ohio Statehouse: This historic building in Columbus offers tours and exhibits on the state's political history.
- Pro Football Hall of Fame: Situated in Canton, it celebrates the history and achievements of professional football.

Cuisine

Ohio's culinary scene is a blend of traditional Midwestern comfort food and innovative dining. Classic dishes include Cincinnati chili, pierogies in Cleveland, and Buckeyes, a peanut butter and chocolate treat.

Literature and Arts

Ohio has also been home to notable literary figures such as Sherwood Anderson, Toni Morrison, and James Thurber. The state's museums, including the Cleveland Museum of Art and the Cincinnati Art Museum, offer world-class collections.

The history and culture of Ohio reflect its pivotal role in shaping the nation, with a legacy of innovation, resilience, and creativity that continues to thrive today.

CHAPTER 3: TOP DESTINATIONS

Columbus: The Capital City

Columbus, the capital city of Ohio, is a vibrant and dynamic metropolis that offers a perfect blend of culture, innovation, and community spirit. It's a city where history meets modernity, and there's always something new to discover. Here are some highlights and reasons why people love Columbus:

Highlights
- Scioto Mile: This stunning urban oasis along the Scioto River features lush parks, scenic pathways, and striking fountains. It's a perfect spot for a leisurely walk, bike ride, or simply enjoying the picturesque views of the city skyline.
- Short North Arts District: Known as the "art and soul" of Columbus, the Short North is brimming with art galleries, boutiques, and vibrant murals.

The district comes alive during the Gallery Hop, a monthly event where galleries and businesses open their doors for an evening of art, music, and culture.
- North Market: A food lover's paradise, North Market is a bustling public market that offers a diverse range of local and international cuisines. From fresh produce to artisanal goods, there's something to satisfy every palate.
- Columbus Zoo and Aquarium: One of the top-rated zoos in the country, the Columbus Zoo is home to a wide variety of animals and exhibits. It's a great family-friendly destination that also features an adjoining water park, Zoombezi Bay.
- Ohio State University: A major educational institution, OSU's campus is a hub of activity with beautiful green spaces, sporting events, and cultural attractions. The university's Wexner Center for the Arts is renowned for its contemporary art exhibitions and performances.
- German Village: This historic neighborhood is known for its charming brick streets, beautifully restored homes, and cozy cafes. A visit to German Village isn't complete without stopping by Schiller Park or enjoying a meal at the famous Schmidt's Sausage Haus.
- COSI (Center of Science and Industry): This interactive science museum offers hands-on exhibits and live shows that are both educational and entertaining for visitors of all ages.

What People Love About Columbus
- Welcoming Community: Columbus is known for its friendly and inclusive atmosphere. The city prides itself on its diverse population and strong sense of community.
- Cultural Diversity: With a rich tapestry of cultures, Columbus celebrates its diversity through festivals, culinary experiences, and cultural institutions. Events like the Columbus Arts Festival and the Asian Festival highlight the city's multicultural spirit.
- Innovation and Growth: Columbus is a city on the rise, with a growing tech scene and a focus on innovation. The city is home to numerous startups, tech companies, and research institutions, making it an exciting place for entrepreneurs and creatives.
- Sports Enthusiasm: Residents are passionate about their sports, especially college football. The Ohio State Buckeyes games at Ohio Stadium create an electrifying atmosphere that brings the community together.
- Green Spaces: Columbus boasts a wealth of parks and recreational areas, offering residents and visitors plenty of opportunities to enjoy the outdoors. In addition to the Scioto Mile, the Franklin Park Conservatory and Botanical Gardens is a favorite for nature enthusiasts.
- Arts and Entertainment: From theaters and galleries to live music venues and festivals, Columbus has a thriving arts and entertainment

scene. The city's commitment to supporting the arts is evident in its numerous cultural events and institutions.

Columbus is a city that continually evolves while maintaining its unique character and charm. Whether you're exploring its historic neighborhoods, enjoying its culinary delights, or engaging in its vibrant cultural scene, Columbus offers an unforgettable experience that keeps visitors coming back for more.

Cleveland: On the Shores of Lake Erie

Cleveland, perched on the southern shore of Lake Erie, is a city that beautifully combines a rich industrial past with a vibrant, modern cultural scene. Known for its iconic landmarks, thriving arts community, and passionate sports fans, Cleveland offers a variety of experiences for visitors.

Highlights
- Rock and Roll Hall of Fame: This world-renowned museum is a must-visit for music lovers. Located on the lakefront, it celebrates the history and impact of rock music and features exhibits on legendary artists and bands.
- Cleveland Museum of Art: One of the most comprehensive art museums in the United States, it houses an impressive collection spanning thousands of years and numerous cultures. The museum's stunning architecture and beautiful gardens make it a serene place to explore.
- West Side Market: A Cleveland institution since 1912, this historic market is a food lover's paradise. With over 100 vendors selling fresh produce, meats, baked goods, and international cuisine, it's a fantastic spot to sample local flavors.
- Cuyahoga Valley National Park: Just a short drive from downtown, this national park offers scenic beauty and outdoor recreation. Visitors can hike, bike, and enjoy the serene landscapes along the Towpath Trail and Brandywine Falls.
- Playhouse Square: The largest performing arts center outside of New York City, Playhouse Square is home to nine theaters hosting Broadway shows, concerts, and other live performances. Its beautifully restored theaters make it a cultural gem in the heart of Cleveland.

- Cleveland Metroparks: Known as the "Emerald Necklace," this extensive network of parks surrounds the city and provides numerous opportunities for outdoor activities, including hiking, fishing, and picnicking.
- Lake Erie Shores: Cleveland's waterfront offers beautiful views and recreational opportunities. Visit Edgewater Park for sandy beaches, swimming, and picnicking, or take a stroll along the Cleveland Lakefront Nature Preserve.

What People Love About Cleveland
- Cultural Diversity: Cleveland's neighborhoods each have their own unique character and cultural heritage. Areas like Little Italy, Tremont, and Ohio City offer diverse culinary experiences and vibrant community events.
- Passionate Sports Fans: The city is home to devoted fans and iconic sports teams, including the Cleveland Browns (NFL), Cleveland Cavaliers (NBA), and Cleveland Guardians (MLB). Game days bring a palpable energy and camaraderie among residents.
- Innovation and Revival: Cleveland has undergone significant revitalization in recent years, with new developments in the downtown area, the revitalization of the Flats East Bank, and a growing tech and healthcare sector.
- Festivals and Events: The city hosts a variety of festivals throughout the year, celebrating everything from music and arts to food and

cultural heritage. Notable events include the Cleveland International Film Festival, IngenuityFest, and the Feast of the Assumption.
- Culinary Scene: Cleveland's food scene is thriving, with a mix of classic comfort food and innovative dining. Local favorites include pierogies, Polish Boy sandwiches, and artisanal ice cream from shops like Mitchell's.
- Historic Charm: From the historic architecture of the Warehouse District to the beautiful old homes in Shaker Heights, Cleveland's history is preserved and celebrated throughout the city.

Cleveland is a city that captivates with its blend of tradition and modernity, its rich cultural offerings, and its friendly, welcoming community. Whether you're exploring its museums, enjoying a game, or simply taking in the lakeside views, Cleveland is a destination that leaves a lasting impression.

Cincinnati: The Queen City

Cincinnati, affectionately known as "The Queen City," is a vibrant and historic metropolis nestled on the northern banks of the Ohio River. This city is known for its rich cultural heritage, stunning architecture, and lively community spirit. Here are some highlights and reasons why people love Cincinnati:

Highlights
- Over-the-Rhine (OTR): This historic district is a gem of 19th-century architecture, featuring beautifully restored buildings, trendy boutiques, and a dynamic food and drink scene. Don't miss Findlay Market, Ohio's oldest continuously operated public market, offering fresh produce and local delicacies.
- Cincinnati Zoo & Botanical Garden: One of the oldest zoos in the United States, it's home to a vast array of animals and beautiful gardens. The zoo is famous for its successful breeding programs and educational exhibits, making it a great destination for families.
- The Banks: This riverfront development is a hub of activity, with parks, eateries, and entertainment venues. Smale Riverfront Park offers scenic views, playgrounds, and walking trails along the Ohio River, while nearby Great American Ball Park is home to the Cincinnati Reds, the city's Major League Baseball team.

- Cincinnati Art Museum: Located in the picturesque Eden Park, the museum boasts an extensive collection of art from around the world. Admission is free, making it accessible for everyone to enjoy.
- Fountain Square: Often considered the heart of downtown Cincinnati, Fountain Square is a lively gathering place for concerts, events, and dining. The Tyler Davidson Fountain, a striking centerpiece, adds to the square's charm.
- Cincinnati Music Hall: This grand venue is an architectural marvel and home to the Cincinnati Symphony Orchestra, Cincinnati Opera, and May Festival. Its ornate design and rich acoustics make it a cultural treasure.
- Krohn Conservatory: Nestled in Eden Park, this conservatory features a stunning collection of exotic plants and seasonal floral shows. It's a serene escape within the city.

What People Love About Cincinnati
- Cultural Diversity: Cincinnati celebrates its diverse cultural heritage with various festivals and events. The city's German roots are evident in its Oktoberfest Zinzinnati, one of the largest in the U.S., while the Cincinnati Hispanic Festival and Asian Food Fest highlight its multicultural spirit.
- Culinary Scene: The Queen City is renowned for its unique culinary offerings. Cincinnati chili, served over spaghetti with a mountain of cheese,

is a local favorite. The city's burgeoning craft beer scene, with numerous breweries, also attracts beer enthusiasts.
- Sports Enthusiasm: Cincinnatians are passionate about their sports teams. The Cincinnati Bengals (NFL) and the Cincinnati Reds (MLB) have dedicated fan bases, and game days bring a buzz of excitement throughout the city.
- Beautiful Parks: Cincinnati boasts an impressive network of parks and green spaces. From the urban oasis of Washington Park in OTR to the scenic beauty of Mount Airy Forest, there are plenty of opportunities to enjoy the outdoors.
- Historic Charm: The city's neighborhoods, each with its own character, offer a blend of historic charm and modern amenities. Areas like Hyde Park, Mount Adams, and Walnut Hills showcase beautiful architecture and quaint streets.
- Community Spirit: Cincinnati is known for its strong sense of community and friendly residents. The city's festivals, farmers' markets, and community events foster a welcoming and inclusive atmosphere.

Cincinnati is a city that beautifully balances its rich history with a forward-thinking attitude. Whether you're exploring its cultural institutions, enjoying its culinary delights, or taking in a game, Cincinnati offers a unique and memorable experience that truly captures the essence of the Queen City.

Dayton: The Birthplace of Aviation

Dayton, Ohio, is famously known as the "Birthplace of Aviation," and for good reason. This city holds a pivotal place in aviation history and offers a variety of attractions that celebrate its rich heritage. Here's what makes Dayton a standout destination:

Highlights
- National Museum of the United States Air Force: As the world's oldest and largest military aviation museum, this incredible facility boasts over 360 aircraft and missiles on display. From the Wright brothers' early gliders to modern stealth aircraft, it's a treasure trove of aviation history. The Presidential Gallery, featuring aircraft used by American presidents, is a highlight.
- Wright Brothers National Museum: Located within Carillon Historical Park, this museum offers a comprehensive look at the lives and achievements of Wilbur and Orville Wright. It

includes the original 1905 Wright Flyer III, the only airplane designated a National Historic Landmark.
- Carillon Historical Park: This 65-acre park showcases Dayton's rich history with exhibits on the city's industrial and technological innovations. In addition to the Wright Brothers National Museum, visitors can explore historic buildings, antique automobiles, and the beautiful Deeds Carillon, a 151-foot-tall bell tower.
- Boonshoft Museum of Discovery: Perfect for families, this interactive science center features a wide range of exhibits on natural history, anthropology, and space. The museum's planetarium and live animal exhibits are popular attractions.
- Dayton Aviation Heritage National Historical Park: This park preserves several sites linked to the Wright brothers and their early aviation experiments. Key locations include the Wright Cycle Company, where they built their first bicycles and airplanes, and the Huffman Prairie Flying Field, where they perfected their flying techniques.
- Dayton Art Institute: An architectural gem, this museum houses an impressive collection of fine art, ranging from ancient artifacts to contemporary works. The museum also offers stunning views of the city and the Great Miami River from its perch on a hill.

What People Love About Dayton
- Rich Aviation History: Dayton's deep connection to aviation history is a major draw for visitors. The city's museums and historical sites provide a fascinating look into the pioneering work of the Wright brothers and the development of flight.
- Educational Attractions: Dayton is home to several educational and interactive museums that engage visitors of all ages. From the immersive exhibits at the National Museum of the United States Air Force to the hands-on displays at the Boonshoft Museum, there's plenty to learn and explore.
- Community Spirit: Daytonians are known for their friendliness and community pride. The city hosts numerous events and festivals throughout the year that bring people together, fostering a strong sense of local camaraderie.
- Scenic Parks and Outdoor Spaces: The city offers a wealth of parks and recreational areas, such as the Five Rivers MetroParks, which provide opportunities for hiking, biking, and enjoying nature. RiverScape MetroPark, located downtown along the Great Miami River, is a popular spot for picnics, concerts, and outdoor activities.
- Culinary Scene: Dayton's food scene is diverse and vibrant, with an array of dining options that range from classic American fare to international cuisine. Local favorites include craft breweries, farm-to-table restaurants, and historic eateries

like the Pine Club, known for its legendary steaks.
- Arts and Culture: Dayton has a thriving arts community, with venues like the Schuster Performing Arts Center offering a variety of performances, from Broadway shows to concerts by the Dayton Philharmonic Orchestra. The city's cultural festivals, such as the Dayton Celtic Festival and the Dayton Greek Festival, celebrate its diverse heritage.

Dayton is a city that beautifully melds its rich historical legacy with a vibrant, modern cultural scene. Whether you're an aviation enthusiast, a history buff, or just looking for a welcoming community with plenty to see and do, Dayton offers a unique and memorable experience.

Toledo: The Glass City

Toledo, often referred to as "The Glass City," is a vibrant and industrious city located in northwest Ohio, along the western end of Lake Erie. Known for its rich history in glass manufacturing, Toledo is a city that seamlessly blends its industrial roots with a diverse cultural scene and beautiful natural landscapes.

Highlights

- Toledo Museum of Art: This world-class museum is renowned for its impressive collection of artworks, including a stunning array of glass pieces. The Glass Pavilion, part of the museum, offers visitors a closer look at the art and science of glassblowing with live demonstrations and an extensive glass art collection.
- Toledo Zoo & Aquarium: A beloved attraction, the Toledo Zoo is home to a wide variety of animals and exhibits. The zoo's aquarium, renovated in recent years, features an array of aquatic life from around the world. It's a great destination for families and animal enthusiasts.
- Imagination Station: This hands-on science museum offers interactive exhibits and live demonstrations that make science fun for visitors of all ages. It's an engaging and educational experience that sparks curiosity and creativity.
- Wildwood Preserve Metropark: One of the many beautiful parks in the area, Wildwood Preserve offers scenic trails, historic buildings, and lush

Ohio Travel Guide 2025

landscapes. It's a perfect spot for hiking, picnicking, and enjoying nature.
- Maumee Bay State Park: Located along Lake Erie, this state park offers stunning waterfront views, sandy beaches, and a range of outdoor activities, including hiking, bird-watching, and fishing. The park's lodge and cabins provide a great option for a relaxing stay.
- National Museum of the Great Lakes: This museum provides a comprehensive look at the history of the Great Lakes, featuring exhibits on shipbuilding, shipping, and maritime heritage. It includes the museum ship S.S. Col. James M. Schoonmaker, which visitors can explore.

What People Love About Toledo
- Glass Heritage: Toledo's nickname, "The Glass City," stems from its historical significance in the glass industry. The city has been a leader in glass manufacturing since the late 19th century, and its legacy is celebrated through attractions like the Toledo Museum of Art's Glass Pavilion and various glass studios.
- Cultural Diversity: Toledo is a melting pot of cultures, reflected in its festivals, food, and community events. The Toledo Opera, Toledo Symphony Orchestra, and various cultural festivals, such as the Greek-American Festival and German-American Festival, showcase the city's rich cultural tapestry.

- Sports Enthusiasm: Toledoans are passionate about their sports teams. The city is home to the Toledo Mud Hens, a minor league baseball team with a devoted following, and the Toledo Walleye, a professional ice hockey team. The Huntington Center and Fifth Third Field are popular venues for sports and entertainment events.
- Educational Institutions: The University of Toledo is a major educational institution in the city, offering a range of academic programs and contributing to the vibrant campus life. The university also hosts various cultural and athletic events.
- Historic Architecture: Toledo boasts beautiful historic buildings and neighborhoods, such as the Old West End, which features one of the largest collections of late Victorian and Edwardian homes in the United States. The area's annual Old West End Festival celebrates this architectural heritage.
- Community Spirit: Toledo's residents are known for their friendliness and community pride. The city's numerous volunteer organizations, neighborhood associations, and community events foster a strong sense of belonging and collaboration.

Toledo is a city that takes pride in its past while looking forward to the future. Whether you're exploring its rich glass heritage, enjoying its cultural offerings, or relaxing in its beautiful parks, Toledo offers a unique and memorable experience that truly captures the spirit of The Glass City.

CHAPTER 4: OUTDOOR ADVENTURES

Hiking at Hocking Hills State Park

Hocking Hills State Park, located in southeastern Ohio, is a haven for nature lovers and outdoor enthusiasts. With its stunning landscapes, diverse trails, and serene atmosphere, it offers a perfect escape into nature. Here's what you can expect when hiking at Hocking Hills State Park:

Things People Will Love
- Breathtaking Scenery: The park is renowned for its picturesque cliffs, waterfalls, gorges, and lush forests. The natural beauty of Hocking Hills provides a tranquil and awe-inspiring hiking experience.
- Diverse Trails: There are trails for all skill levels, from easy walks to more challenging hikes. Each

trail offers unique views and geological features, ensuring a memorable adventure for everyone.
- Wildlife: Hocking Hills is home to a variety of wildlife, including deer, birds, and smaller mammals. Nature enthusiasts will enjoy the opportunity to observe these animals in their natural habitat.
- Photography Opportunities: The park's stunning landscapes provide countless photo opportunities. Whether you're a professional photographer or just love capturing nature's beauty, Hocking Hills won't disappoint.

Key Highlights
- Old Man's Cave: One of the most popular destinations in the park, Old Man's Cave features a series of beautiful waterfalls, rock formations, and a scenic gorge. It's named after a hermit who lived in the cave in the 1800s.
- Ash Cave: This large recess cave is the largest of its kind in Ohio. The easy trail to Ash Cave is accessible and leads to a stunning waterfall that cascades into a small pool.
- Cedar Falls: Known for its powerful waterfall, Cedar Falls is a favorite spot for visitors. The trail to the falls winds through a beautiful forested area, adding to the scenic experience.
- Rock House: This unique cave features natural "windows" carved into the rock, providing a fascinating exploration experience. The Rock

House trail is slightly more challenging but rewarding with its distinctive features.
- Cantwell Cliffs: Located in the northern part of the park, Cantwell Cliffs offers dramatic cliffs and a deep gorge. The trail here is known for its rugged beauty and panoramic views.

Safety Tips
- Stay on Marked Trails: To ensure your safety and protect the natural environment, always stay on the designated trails. Straying off the path can lead to accidents or damage to the ecosystem.
- Wear Appropriate Footwear: The trails can be uneven and slippery, especially near waterfalls. Sturdy, comfortable hiking shoes with good grip are essential.
- Bring Plenty of Water: Staying hydrated is crucial, especially during longer hikes or on hot days. Carry enough water for your hike and drink regularly.
- Check the Weather: Before heading out, check the weather forecast. Be prepared for changing conditions, and avoid hiking during severe weather.
- Pack Essentials: Bring a map of the park, a first-aid kit, snacks, and a fully charged phone. It's also a good idea to let someone know your hiking plans and expected return time.
- Respect Wildlife: Observe animals from a distance and do not feed them. Keep the park

clean by carrying out all trash and following Leave No Trace principles.
- Use Caution Near Waterfalls and Cliffs: Be careful when near edges and slippery surfaces. Never climb on waterfalls or rock formations, as they can be unstable and dangerous.

Hocking Hills State Park offers an unforgettable hiking experience with its stunning natural beauty and diverse trails. Whether you're exploring its famous caves, marveling at waterfalls, or enjoying the serenity of the forest, Hocking Hills is a true gem for outdoor adventurers.

Kayaking on Lake Erie

Kayaking on Lake Erie offers an incredible opportunity to experience one of North America's Great Lakes from a unique perspective. Whether you're a seasoned kayaker or a beginner, the vast expanse of Lake Erie provides a perfect backdrop for a memorable adventure. Here are some highlights and tips to make the most of your kayaking experience on Lake Erie:

Things People Will Love
- Scenic Beauty: Lake Erie is surrounded by stunning landscapes, from sandy beaches and rocky shores to picturesque islands. Kayaking allows you to explore these beautiful areas up close and at your own pace.
- Wildlife Viewing: The lake and its surroundings are home to a variety of wildlife, including birds, fish, and even the occasional turtle. Kayaking offers a serene way to observe these creatures in their natural habitats.
- Peaceful Escape: The gentle lapping of the water and the open expanse of the lake create a tranquil and relaxing environment, perfect for unwinding and connecting with nature.

Key Highlights
- Lake Erie Islands: The lake is dotted with several islands, each offering unique attractions. Popular destinations include Put-in-Bay on South Bass Island, Kelleys Island, and Middle Bass Island. These islands feature charming towns, historic sites, and beautiful natural areas that are perfect for exploration by kayak.

- Coastal Wetlands: Areas like the Magee Marsh Wildlife Area and the Ottawa National Wildlife Refuge are renowned for their wetlands and marshes. Kayaking through these regions provides an excellent opportunity for bird watching and experiencing the rich biodiversity of the area.
- Presque Isle State Park: Located in Pennsylvania, this park features a 3,200-acre peninsula that extends into Lake Erie. It's a popular destination for kayaking, with its lagoons, coves, and sandy beaches offering plenty of opportunities for exploration.
- Lake Erie Bluffs: This park in Ohio features high shale cliffs that provide breathtaking views of the lake. Kayaking along the base of these cliffs offers a unique perspective of the dramatic landscape.

Safety Tips
- Check the Weather: Lake Erie can be subject to rapidly changing weather conditions. Always check the weather forecast before heading out and be prepared for changes. Avoid kayaking during storms or high winds.
- Wear a Life Jacket: Safety is paramount, and wearing a properly fitted life jacket is essential for all kayakers, regardless of skill level.
- Know Your Limits: Be aware of your kayaking experience and skill level. Choose routes and areas that match your abilities. If you're a

- beginner, consider going with a guide or joining a kayaking tour.
- Stay Hydrated and Protected: Bring plenty of water and stay hydrated, especially on sunny days. Use sunscreen and wear a hat and sunglasses to protect yourself from the sun.
- Buddy System: If possible, kayak with a partner or a group. It's always safer to have someone with you in case of an emergency.
- Emergency Supplies: Carry a small waterproof bag with essential supplies, such as a whistle, a first-aid kit, a flashlight, and a fully charged phone in case of emergencies.
- Follow Local Regulations: Be aware of and follow any local boating regulations and guidelines. Some areas may have specific rules for kayakers.

Kayaking on Lake Erie is a fantastic way to explore the natural beauty of the region, enjoy some peaceful time on the water, and experience the lake's diverse ecosystems. Whether you're paddling around the islands, gliding through coastal wetlands, or enjoying the stunning views from the bluffs, Lake Erie offers a kayaking adventure you won't soon forget.

Rock Climbing at John Bryan State Park

John Bryan State Park, located in western Ohio near Yellow Springs, is a popular destination for outdoor enthusiasts, particularly rock climbers. The park's natural limestone cliffs and scenic trails offer an ideal setting for both experienced climbers and those new to the sport. Here's what makes rock climbing at John Bryan State Park a fantastic experience:

Things People Will Love
- Scenic Beauty: The park is renowned for its picturesque landscapes, featuring rugged cliffs, dense forests, and the Little Miami River. The natural beauty of the area provides a stunning backdrop for climbing adventures.
- Variety of Climbing Routes: The limestone cliffs in the park offer a range of climbing routes that cater to different skill levels. Whether you're a novice or an experienced climber, there's a route that will challenge and excite you.

- Close Proximity to Nature: Climbing at John Bryan State Park allows you to connect deeply with nature. The park's trails and climbing areas are surrounded by wildlife and lush vegetation, providing a peaceful and immersive outdoor experience.

Key Highlights
- Limestone Cliffs: The park's cliffs are composed of high-quality limestone, providing excellent grip and a range of climbing features, such as cracks, ledges, and overhangs.
- The Cliffs Area: One of the most popular climbing spots in the park, The Cliffs Area, offers various routes that range from easy to challenging. This area is perfect for both top-rope climbing and bouldering.
- Yellow Springs: After a day of climbing, you can explore the charming nearby village of Yellow Springs. Known for its artistic community, unique shops, and local eateries, it's a great place to unwind and enjoy a meal.

Safety Tips
- Use Proper Gear: Ensure you have the right climbing equipment, including a helmet, harness, climbing shoes, and a belay device. Double-check your gear before each climb.
- Climb with a Partner: It's always safer to climb with a partner who can belay for you and provide assistance if needed. Never climb alone.

- Check Weather Conditions: Before heading out, check the weather forecast. Avoid climbing during or after rain, as wet rocks can be slippery and dangerous.
- Follow Park Rules: Adhere to all park regulations and guidelines. Some areas may have specific rules regarding climbing to protect the natural environment.
- Stay Hydrated and Nourished: Bring plenty of water and snacks to keep your energy levels up. Climbing is physically demanding, so staying hydrated and well-nourished is crucial.
- Know Your Limits: Climb within your skill level and don't push yourself beyond your limits. If you're new to climbing, consider taking a class or hiring a guide to ensure you're using proper techniques.
- Respect Wildlife: Be mindful of the local wildlife and natural environment. Leave no trace and carry out all trash to help preserve the park's beauty.
- Emergency Plan: Have a plan in place in case of emergencies. Carry a first-aid kit and a fully charged phone, and know the location of the nearest help or ranger station.

Rock climbing at John Bryan State Park is an exhilarating way to experience the great outdoors and challenge yourself physically and mentally. With its diverse routes, stunning scenery, and peaceful surroundings, it's a perfect destination for climbers of all levels.

Zip Lining at Mohican State Park

Mohican State Park, nestled in the heart of Ohio, is a popular destination for outdoor enthusiasts, offering a variety of activities including hiking, canoeing, and fishing. One of the most exhilarating experiences at Mohican is zip lining, which provides a thrilling way to explore the park's stunning landscapes from above.

Things People Will Love
- Bird's-Eye View: Zip lining offers a unique perspective of the park's beautiful scenery, allowing you to soar above the trees and enjoy panoramic views of the forest, river, and valleys.

- Adrenaline Rush: For thrill-seekers, zip lining provides an exciting adventure that combines speed, height, and stunning surroundings.
- Nature Immersion: This activity gives you the chance to connect with nature in an extraordinary way, gliding through the treetops and experiencing the sights and sounds of the forest from a new vantage point.

Key Highlights
- Multiple Zip Lines: The zip lining course at Mohican State Park features multiple zip lines of varying lengths and heights, providing an exciting and diverse experience for participants.
- Scenic Views: As you zip through the course, you'll have breathtaking views of the Clear Fork Gorge, the Mohican River, and the dense woodland that makes the park so picturesque.
- Guided Tours: Experienced guides lead the zip lining tours, ensuring your safety and providing interesting information about the park's history, flora, and fauna. Their expertise enhances the overall experience, making it both educational and fun.
- Canopy Walks: Some zip line tours include canopy walks, which allow you to traverse suspension bridges high above the forest floor, adding another layer of adventure to your outing.

Safety Tips
- Follow Instructions: Always listen to and follow the instructions provided by your guides. They are trained professionals who prioritize your safety and enjoyment.
- Wear Appropriate Gear: Make sure to wear comfortable clothing and closed-toe shoes. The zip lining facility will provide essential safety gear, including helmets and harnesses.
- Stay Hydrated: Bring water and stay hydrated, especially on hot days. Zip lining can be physically demanding, so it's important to take care of your body.
- Check Weather Conditions: Zip lining is weather-dependent, so check the forecast before your visit. Tours may be postponed or canceled in case of severe weather conditions for safety reasons.
- Health Considerations: If you have any medical conditions or concerns, consult with your doctor before participating. Ensure you are in good physical condition to handle the activity.
- Secure Personal Belongings: Make sure to secure any loose items before starting the zip line. It's best to leave valuables in a safe place to avoid losing them during the activity.
- Stay Calm and Enjoy: If you're nervous, take deep breaths and focus on the beautiful surroundings. Trust in the safety measures and enjoy the ride!

Zip lining at Mohican State Park is an unforgettable adventure that combines the thrill of flying with the beauty of nature. Whether you're an adrenaline junkie or simply looking to try something new, zip lining at Mohican offers a memorable experience that will leave you wanting more.

CHAPTER 5: SCENIC ROUTES AND ROAD TRIPS

Ohio River Scenic Byway

The Ohio River Scenic Byway is a picturesque route that stretches along the Ohio River, offering travelers a glimpse into the rich history, charming small towns, and beautiful landscapes of the region. This scenic byway extends through three states: Ohio, Indiana, and Illinois, with the Ohio segment providing particularly captivating views and cultural experiences.

Key Highlights
- Historic Towns: The byway passes through several historic towns that are brimming with charm and character. Places like Marietta, the first permanent settlement in the Northwest

Territory, and Gallipolis, founded by French immigrants, offer a wealth of historical sites and quaint downtown areas to explore.
- Bluff Views: The route features numerous overlooks that provide stunning views of the Ohio River and its surrounding bluffs. These scenic spots are perfect for photography, picnics, or simply taking in the natural beauty of the region.
- Marietta Earthworks: In Marietta, you can find ancient earthworks and mounds built by the prehistoric Hopewell and Adena cultures. The Mound Cemetery is home to one of the largest conical mounds in the state.
- Belpre's Blennerhassett Island: Just across the river from Belpre, Ohio, this island is known for its historical significance and beautiful landscapes. Visitors can take a sternwheeler riverboat to the island and tour the reconstructed Blennerhassett Mansion.
- Ohio River Islands National Wildlife Refuge: This refuge includes several islands along the Ohio River, offering excellent opportunities for bird watching, wildlife observation, and enjoying the natural environment.
- Ripley: Known for its pivotal role in the Underground Railroad, Ripley features significant historical sites like the John Rankin House and the John Parker House, where freedom seekers were given shelter on their journey to freedom.

What People Love About the Ohio River Scenic Byway
- Rich History: Travelers love the deep historical significance of the towns and landmarks along the byway. From prehistoric mounds to pivotal Civil War and Underground Railroad sites, the route is steeped in history.
- Scenic Beauty: The Ohio River Scenic Byway offers breathtaking views of the Ohio River, lush forests, and rolling hills. The natural beauty of the area is a major draw for those seeking a peaceful and picturesque drive.
- Small Town Charm: The byway is dotted with charming small towns, each with its unique character and hospitality. Visitors enjoy exploring local shops, dining at quaint restaurants, and experiencing the friendly atmosphere of these communities.
- Cultural Experiences: The route offers a variety of cultural experiences, including museums, historic homes, and festivals. These cultural attractions provide insights into the local heritage and traditions of the region.
- Outdoor Activities: The byway provides plenty of opportunities for outdoor recreation, such as hiking, bird watching, fishing, and boating. The Ohio River and its surrounding landscapes offer numerous spots for outdoor enthusiasts to enjoy.
- Relaxed Pace: Travelers appreciate the leisurely pace of the drive, allowing them to take their

time exploring each destination along the route. It's a perfect way to unwind and enjoy a scenic road trip.

The Ohio River Scenic Byway is a journey through time and nature, offering a blend of historical exploration, cultural enrichment, and stunning landscapes. Whether you're interested in history, outdoor activities, or simply enjoying a scenic drive, this byway provides a memorable and enriching experience.

Amish Country Byways

The Amish Country Byways provide a serene and scenic journey through the heart of Ohio's Amish communities. This picturesque route weaves through rolling hills, verdant farmlands, and charming villages, offering travelers a glimpse into a simpler, more traditional way of life. Here's what makes the Amish Country Byways an exceptional and memorable experience:

Key Highlights
- Berlin: One of the main hubs in Ohio's Amish Country, Berlin is known for its charming shops, bakeries, and craft stores. It's a great place to sample Amish pastries, shop for quilts, and enjoy local dining.
- Sugarcreek: Often referred to as the "Little Switzerland of Ohio," Sugarcreek combines Swiss heritage with Amish culture. Don't miss the world's largest cuckoo clock, a delightful attraction in the town square.
- Walnut Creek: This village offers a range of attractions, including the Amish Country Theater, which features family-friendly entertainment, and Walnut Creek Cheese, a popular stop for local cheeses and gourmet foods.
- Millersburg: The historic downtown area of Millersburg is known for its antique shops, the Victorian House Museum, and the Holmes County Courthouse. It's a charming place to explore and soak in the local history.
- Mt. Hope: Home to Mt. Hope Auction, this village hosts weekly livestock and produce auctions, providing a fascinating insight into the local agricultural community.
- Yoder's Amish Home: Located near Walnut Creek, Yoder's Amish Home offers guided tours of a traditional Amish homestead, giving visitors an authentic look at Amish daily life, farming practices, and craftsmanship.

What People Love About the Amish Country Byways

- Authentic Experience: Visitors appreciate the authentic and respectful immersion into Amish culture. The byways provide a unique opportunity to see and experience the simplicity and dedication of the Amish way of life.
- Handcrafted Goods: The quality and craftsmanship of the Amish-made products are highly valued. From furniture and quilts to baked goods and jams, the attention to detail and tradition is evident in every item.
- Delicious Food: Amish Country is known for its hearty and delicious cuisine. Many visitors enjoy the homestyle cooking found in local restaurants and bakeries, including pies, bread, cheese, and home-cooked meals.
- Hospitality: The friendly and welcoming nature of the Amish and local communities adds to the charm of the byways. Visitors often remark on the kindness and warmth they experience while exploring the area.
- Slower Pace: The peaceful and unhurried pace of life in Amish Country provides a refreshing contrast to the hustle and bustle of modern life. It's a perfect destination for those looking to relax and unwind.

The Amish Country Byways offer a serene and enriching journey through one of Ohio's most unique and culturally rich regions. Whether you're enjoying the scenic drives, exploring charming villages, or experiencing the warmth of Amish hospitality, the byways provide a memorable and authentic travel experience.

Lake Erie Coastal Trail

The Lake Erie Coastal Trail is a scenic byway that runs along the southern shore of Lake Erie, offering breathtaking views, charming coastal towns, and a wealth of outdoor activities. This picturesque route is perfect for those looking to explore Ohio's beautiful lakefront and enjoy a variety of recreational opportunities. Here's what makes the Lake Erie Coastal Trail an exceptional travel experience:

Key Highlights
- Cleveland: Start your journey in Cleveland, where you can visit the famous Rock and Roll Hall of Fame, the Cleveland Museum of Art, and enjoy waterfront dining at the Flats East Bank. The city's vibrant culture and attractions set the tone for a memorable trip along the coast.
- Edgewater Park: Located just west of downtown Cleveland, Edgewater Park offers stunning views of Lake Erie, sandy beaches, picnic areas, and walking trails. It's a great spot to relax and enjoy the lake's beauty.
- Lorain: Known for its historic lighthouse, Lorain offers beautiful views of the lake and access to recreational activities like boating and fishing. The Lorain Harbor is a popular spot for watching sunsets over the water.
- Vermilion: This quaint town is often called the "Village of Lake Captains" due to its rich maritime history. Explore the charming downtown area, visit the Vermilion Lighthouse, and take a leisurely stroll along the beach.
- Sandusky: Home to the renowned Cedar Point amusement park, Sandusky is a hub of excitement and fun. Besides the thrill rides, you can enjoy waterfront dining, boat tours, and a visit to the Merry-Go-Round Museum.
- Marblehead Lighthouse State Park: This park features the oldest continuously operating lighthouse on the Great Lakes. The Marblehead Lighthouse offers stunning views of Lake Erie

and the surrounding area, making it a must-see stop on your journey.
- Put-in-Bay: Take a ferry from Catawba Island or Port Clinton to South Bass Island, where you'll find the lively village of Put-in-Bay. The island offers a variety of attractions, including wineries, caves, and the Perry's Victory and International Peace Memorial.
- Kelleys Island: Another gem of Lake Erie, Kelleys Island is known for its natural beauty and laid-back atmosphere. Explore the island's glacial grooves, hike through the nature preserves, and relax on the beaches.
- Maumee Bay State Park: Located near Toledo, this state park offers a mix of recreational activities, including hiking, bird-watching, and swimming. The park's lodge and cabins provide a comfortable place to stay while enjoying the scenic views of the lake.

What People Love About the Lake Erie Coastal Trail
- Stunning Lake Views: The trail offers continuous views of Lake Erie's sparkling waters and picturesque shoreline. Whether driving, biking, or walking, the beauty of the lake is always a highlight.
- Diverse Attractions: From lively cities and historic lighthouses to charming small towns and pristine nature preserves, the Lake Erie Coastal

Trail offers a wide range of attractions that cater to different interests.
- Outdoor Recreation: The trail provides ample opportunities for outdoor activities such as hiking, biking, boating, fishing, and bird-watching. The parks and beaches along the route are perfect for enjoying nature.
- Cultural and Historical Sites: The trail passes by numerous cultural and historical sites, including museums, lighthouses, and historic towns. These sites offer insights into the region's rich heritage and maritime history.
- Family-Friendly Fun: With attractions like Cedar Point, beaches, and nature parks, the Lake Erie Coastal Trail is ideal for family trips. There's something for everyone to enjoy, from thrilling rides to peaceful picnics.
- Relaxing Vibe: The coastal trail's serene landscapes and charming towns provide a relaxing and peaceful atmosphere, making it a great escape from the hustle and bustle of everyday life.

The Lake Erie Coastal Trail is a scenic and enriching journey that showcases the best of Ohio's northern shoreline. Whether you're drawn by the natural beauty, historical sites, or recreational opportunities, this trail promises an unforgettable adventure along the shores of Lake Erie.

Great Miami Riverway

The Great Miami Riverway is a scenic corridor that spans 99 miles along the Great Miami River, stretching from Sidney to Hamilton in southwestern Ohio. This vibrant trail offers a wide range of recreational activities, historical sites, and charming communities, making it an ideal destination for outdoor enthusiasts and history buffs alike.

Key Highlights
- Great Miami River Recreation Trail: This multi-use trail runs alongside the river and is perfect for walking, jogging, cycling, and rollerblading. The trail connects several towns and cities, providing scenic views of the river and surrounding landscapes.
- Riverfront Parks: The Riverway is dotted with beautiful parks that offer various amenities and activities. RiverScape MetroPark in Dayton features fountains, gardens, and outdoor

concerts, while Island MetroPark offers picnic areas, playgrounds, and canoe rentals.
- Paddling and Fishing: The Great Miami River is a popular spot for paddling, kayaking, and fishing. The calm waters and scenic surroundings make for a peaceful and enjoyable experience. Access points along the river provide convenient entry for water activities.
- Historic Towns: The Riverway passes through several historic towns, each with its unique charm and attractions. Troy, for instance, boasts a vibrant downtown area with antique shops, cafes, and annual events like the Strawberry Festival. Piqua offers historical sites such as the Fort Piqua Plaza and Johnston Farm & Indian Agency.
- Museums and Cultural Sites: The National Museum of the United States Air Force in Dayton is a must-visit, featuring an extensive collection of aircraft and aviation exhibits. The Heritage Center of Dayton Manufacturing & Entrepreneurship showcases the region's rich industrial history.
- Miami Valley Hospitality: The communities along the Riverway are known for their friendly residents and welcoming atmosphere. Local shops, restaurants, and festivals offer a taste of the region's hospitality and culture.

What People Love About the Great Miami Riverway

- Outdoor Recreation: The Riverway provides ample opportunities for outdoor activities, including hiking, biking, paddling, and fishing. The well-maintained trails and parks make it easy to enjoy nature and stay active.
- Scenic Beauty: The natural beauty of the Great Miami River and its surroundings is a major draw. The lush greenery, river views, and picturesque landscapes create a peaceful and inviting environment.
- Community Events: The towns along the Riverway host numerous events and festivals throughout the year, celebrating local culture, history, and traditions. These events provide a fun and engaging way to experience the region.
- Historical Significance: The Riverway is rich in history, with numerous historical sites and museums that offer insights into the area's past. From Native American heritage to the industrial revolution, the region's history is preserved and celebrated.
- Family-Friendly Atmosphere: The Riverway is a great destination for families, with plenty of activities and attractions that cater to all ages. Parks, playgrounds, and educational exhibits ensure a fun and enriching experience for everyone.
- Convenient Access: The interconnected trail system and numerous access points make it easy

to explore the Riverway by foot, bike, or boat. The proximity to several major cities, including Dayton, adds to its accessibility.

The Great Miami Riverway offers a diverse and enriching experience, combining outdoor recreation, historical exploration, and community charm. Whether you're paddling on the river, cycling along the trail, or exploring the historic towns, the Riverway promises an unforgettable adventure in southwestern Ohio.

CHAPTER 6: CULTURAL AND HISTORICAL ATTRACTIONS

Rock & Roll Hall of Fame

The Rock & Roll Hall of Fame, located in Cleveland, Ohio, is a world-renowned institution dedicated to preserving the history and celebrating the impact of rock and roll music. Situated on the shores of Lake Erie, this iconic museum is a must-visit for music enthusiasts and cultural historians alike. Here's an in-depth look at what makes the Rock & Roll Hall of Fame a premier cultural and historical attraction:

Key Highlights
- Architectural Marvel: Designed by the legendary architect I. M. Pei, the Rock & Roll Hall of

Ohio Travel Guide 2025

Fame's unique glass pyramid structure is an architectural landmark. Its striking design and lakefront location make it a standout feature in Cleveland's skyline.
- Exhibits and Collections: The museum's exhibits cover the entire history of rock and roll, from its roots in gospel, blues, and country music to its influence on contemporary genres. Visitors can explore the stories of legendary artists, iconic albums, and significant moments in music history through a vast array of artifacts, memorabilia, and interactive displays.
- Induction Gallery: One of the museum's central attractions is the Hall of Fame itself, which honors the greatest contributors to rock and roll. The Induction Gallery features displays dedicated to inductees, including original manuscripts, instruments, and stage costumes. Interactive kiosks provide detailed information about each inductee's career and achievements.
- The Power of Rock Experience: This immersive exhibit showcases the energy and excitement of rock and roll through a dynamic multimedia presentation. Featuring footage from past induction ceremonies and performances, it offers a thrilling look at the genre's most memorable moments.
- Temporary Exhibits: In addition to its permanent collection, the Rock & Roll Hall of Fame hosts rotating temporary exhibits that delve into specific themes, artists, or periods in

music history. These exhibits provide fresh and engaging perspectives on rock and roll's evolving legacy.
- Music Events and Programs: The museum regularly hosts live performances, lectures, film screenings, and educational programs. These events offer visitors the chance to experience rock and roll in an interactive and engaging way, fostering a deeper appreciation for the music and its cultural impact.

What People Love About the Rock & Roll Hall of Fame

- Comprehensive Music History: The Rock & Roll Hall of Fame offers an in-depth and comprehensive look at the history of rock and roll. Visitors appreciate the extensive collection of artifacts and the detailed storytelling that brings the music's history to life.
- Interactive Experiences: The museum's interactive exhibits and multimedia displays make the experience engaging and memorable. Visitors can listen to classic tracks, watch historic performances, and delve into the stories behind their favorite artists and songs.
- Tribute to Legends: The Induction Gallery and Hall of Fame pay tribute to the most influential figures in rock and roll. Fans enjoy seeing the personal artifacts and learning more about the artists who have shaped the genre.

- Cultural Significance: The museum highlights rock and roll's impact on culture, society, and politics. It explores how the music has reflected and influenced social movements and historical events, offering a deeper understanding of its significance.
- Vibrant Atmosphere: The lively and energetic atmosphere of the museum, combined with its stunning architecture and lakefront setting, creates a unique and enjoyable visitor experience. The passion for rock and roll is palpable throughout the museum.

Tips for Visiting
- Plan Ahead: Check the museum's website for current exhibits, events, and ticket information. Planning your visit in advance can help you make the most of your time at the museum.
- Allow Ample Time: The Rock & Roll Hall of Fame is extensive, and there is much to see and experience. Allocate several hours to explore the exhibits thoroughly.
- Engage with Interactive Displays: Take advantage of the museum's interactive elements, such as listening stations, video screens, and touch screens, to enhance your visit.
- Attend Special Events: If possible, time your visit to coincide with a live performance, lecture, or special event. These programs add an extra layer of excitement and engagement to your experience.

- Visit the Museum Store: The museum store offers a wide range of rock and roll-themed merchandise, including books, apparel, and memorabilia. It's a great place to find souvenirs and gifts for music lovers.

The Rock & Roll Hall of Fame is more than just a museum; it's a celebration of the music that has defined generations and shaped culture worldwide. Whether you're a lifelong fan of rock and roll or simply curious about its history, the Rock & Roll Hall of Fame provides an immersive and inspiring journey through the world of music.

National Museum of the US Air Force

The National Museum of the United States Air Force, located at Wright-Patterson Air Force Base near Dayton, Ohio, is the world's oldest and largest military aviation museum. With its extensive collection of aircraft, missiles, and exhibits, the museum offers a comprehensive and immersive experience that appeals to aviation enthusiasts, history buffs, and families alike.

Key Highlights
- Impressive Collection: The museum houses over 360 aircraft and missiles, representing the evolution of aviation from the Wright brothers to modern stealth technology. The collection includes iconic planes like the Wright Flyer, the B-29 Superfortress "Bockscar," and the F-22 Raptor.
- Presidential Gallery: This special gallery features several aircraft used by U.S. presidents, including the Boeing VC-137C SAM 26000, which served as Air Force One for presidents Kennedy through Clinton. Visitors can step inside these historic planes and explore their interiors.
- Space Gallery: The museum's Space Gallery showcases a variety of space-related artifacts, including rockets, satellites, and the Apollo 15 command module. Interactive exhibits and

Ohio Travel Guide 2025

displays provide insights into the history of space exploration and the role of the Air Force in space missions.
- Memorial Park: Located outside the museum, Memorial Park honors the men and women who have served in the United States Air Force. The park features monuments, plaques, and statues commemorating various units, missions, and conflicts.
- Restoration Hangar: Visitors can tour the museum's restoration hangar to see firsthand how aircraft are preserved and restored. This behind-the-scenes look provides a deeper understanding of the meticulous work that goes into maintaining the collection.
- Interactive Exhibits: Throughout the museum, interactive exhibits engage visitors with hands-on activities, flight simulators, and multimedia presentations. These exhibits bring the history of aviation to life and provide an educational experience for all ages.

What People Love About the National Museum of the United States Air Force
- Rich History: The museum's extensive exhibits cover the entire history of aviation and the Air Force, offering a detailed and engaging narrative of technological advancements and historical events.
- Diverse Collection: The wide variety of aircraft and missiles on display allows visitors to explore

different eras and aspects of aviation, from early flight to contemporary aerospace technology.
- Immersive Experience: The opportunity to step inside historic aircraft, explore cockpits, and interact with exhibits creates a truly immersive and memorable experience. Visitors feel connected to the history and stories behind the machines.
- Educational Value: The museum provides a wealth of educational content, making it a fantastic destination for students, families, and anyone interested in learning about aviation and military history. The interactive exhibits and knowledgeable staff enhance the learning experience.
- Free Admission: One of the most appreciated aspects of the museum is that admission is free. This makes it accessible to a wide audience and encourages frequent visits.
- Community and Heritage: The museum fosters a sense of community and pride in the Air Force's heritage. Special events, lectures, and programs bring together veterans, active-duty personnel, and civilians to celebrate and honor aviation history.

Tips for Visiting
- Plan Your Visit: The museum is vast, so plan to spend several hours exploring. Check the museum's website for information on current exhibits, events, and tour schedules.

- Wear Comfortable Shoes: With numerous galleries and hangars to explore, comfortable footwear is essential for an enjoyable visit.
- Check for Special Events: The museum frequently hosts special events, including air shows, lectures, and family activities. Attending these events can enhance your visit.
- Explore the Surroundings: In addition to the museum, Wright-Patterson Air Force Base and the Dayton area offer other aviation-related attractions, such as the Wright Brothers National Museum and Carillon Historical Park.
- Bring a Camera: Photography is allowed, so bring a camera to capture the impressive displays and memorable moments.

The National Museum of the United States Air Force is more than just a museum; it's a tribute to the innovation, bravery, and dedication of the men and women who have contributed to the advancement of aviation. Whether you're an aviation aficionado or a curious visitor, the museum offers an enriching and inspiring journey through the history of flight.

Stan Hywet Hall & Gardens

Stan Hywet Hall & Gardens, located in Akron, Ohio, is one of the largest and most beautifully preserved historic estates in the United States. This stunning property, once the home of industrialist F.A. Seiberling, co-founder of the Goodyear Tire & Rubber Company, offers visitors a captivating journey through history, architecture, and horticulture. Here's an in-depth look at what makes Stan Hywet Hall & Gardens a premier cultural and historical attraction:

Key Highlights
- The Manor House: The centerpiece of the estate, the Manor House, is a magnificent Tudor Revival-style mansion with 65 rooms. Visitors can explore the beautifully furnished rooms, which showcase original furnishings, art, and décor that reflect the elegance and opulence of the early 20th century.
- The Gardens: Spanning 70 acres, the gardens at Stan Hywet are a horticultural delight. Highlights include the English Garden, designed by the renowned landscape architect Ellen Biddle Shipman, the Birch Allee and Vista, the Japanese

Garden, and the Great Garden, which features a stunning array of flowers, shrubs, and ornamental trees.
- The Conservatory: This elegant glass structure houses a variety of tropical plants and seasonal displays. The conservatory offers a serene and beautiful environment for visitors to enjoy year-round.
- The Gate Lodge: This historic building is significant as the site where Alcoholics Anonymous co-founder Dr. Bob Smith had his first meeting with Bill Wilson, the other co-founder of AA. The Gate Lodge now serves as a museum and tribute to this important event in history.
- The Playgarden: Perfect for families, the Playgarden is a whimsical, interactive garden designed for children. It features a range of play structures, water features, and educational elements that encourage exploration and learning.
- Events and Programs: Stan Hywet hosts a variety of events and programs throughout the year, including holiday celebrations, educational workshops, and garden tours. Popular events include the annual Deck the Hall holiday light display and the Ohio Mart arts and crafts festival.

What People Love About Stan Hywet Hall & Gardens
- Architectural Beauty: The Manor House's Tudor Revival architecture and intricate details are a major draw. Visitors appreciate the craftsmanship and historical authenticity of the building, which offers a glimpse into the lifestyle of the early 20th-century elite.
- Stunning Gardens: The meticulously maintained gardens are a highlight for many visitors. The diverse landscapes and plantings provide a beautiful and serene setting that changes with the seasons, making each visit unique.
- Rich History: Stan Hywet's history, from its construction by the Seiberling family to its significance in the founding of Alcoholics Anonymous, adds depth and interest to the visit. The estate's historical significance is well-preserved and thoughtfully presented.
- Educational Value: The estate offers a wealth of educational opportunities, from guided tours and interpretive displays to hands-on workshops and children's programs. Visitors of all ages can learn about history, architecture, gardening, and more.
- Family-Friendly Atmosphere: The Playgarden and family-friendly events make Stan Hywet an ideal destination for visitors with children. The interactive and engaging activities ensure that younger visitors have a memorable and enjoyable experience.

- Seasonal Events: The variety of seasonal events and programs attract repeat visitors. Whether it's the spectacular holiday lights, the spring bloom, or the summer festivals, there's always something new and exciting happening at Stan Hywet.

Tips for Visiting
- Plan Ahead: Check the Stan Hywet Hall & Gardens website for hours of operation, tour schedules, and special event information. Planning your visit in advance can help you make the most of your time at the estate.
- Wear Comfortable Shoes: The estate covers a large area, and there's plenty of walking involved. Comfortable footwear is essential for exploring the house and gardens.
- Bring a Camera: Photography is allowed, and you'll want to capture the beauty of the gardens, the architecture of the Manor House, and the stunning views around the estate.
- Check Event Schedules: If you're interested in attending a special event or program, check the schedule and consider purchasing tickets in advance to ensure availability.
- Explore the Surroundings: Akron and the surrounding area offer additional attractions and dining options. Plan to spend some extra time exploring the region to enhance your visit.

Stan Hywet Hall & Gardens is more than just a historic estate; it's a living museum that celebrates the artistry, culture, and history of the early 20th century. Whether you're strolling through the gardens, touring the grand Manor House, or attending one of the many events, Stan Hywet offers a rich and immersive experience that will leave you inspired and enchanted.

Wright Brothers National Memorial

The Wright Brothers National Memorial, located in Kill Devil Hills, North Carolina, is a site of immense historical significance. This memorial commemorates the achievements of Wilbur and Orville Wright, who made the first successful powered flight on December 17, 190The site offers visitors a deep dive into the history of aviation and the pioneering spirit of the Wright brothers.

Key Highlights
- First Flight Boulder and Markers: The exact location where the Wright brothers made their

historic first flight is marked by a large granite boulder. Nearby, four smaller markers indicate the landing spots of each of the four flights made on that momentous day.
- Wright Brothers Monument: Perched atop Kill Devil Hill, this impressive 60-foot granite monument honors the Wright brothers' contributions to aviation. The climb to the monument offers panoramic views of the surrounding landscape and the Atlantic Ocean, providing a perfect spot for reflection and appreciation.
- Visitor Center: The Visitor Center features exhibits and displays that detail the lives, challenges, and achievements of the Wright brothers. The center includes reproductions of the 1903 Wright Flyer and the 1902 glider, as well as interactive displays that engage visitors of all ages.
- Flight Line: This outdoor exhibit area includes life-size bronze sculptures that recreate the scene of the first flight. The sculptures capture the moment Orville piloted the Wright Flyer with Wilbur running alongside, providing a vivid and immersive experience.
- Park Grounds and Trails: The memorial park includes several walking trails and interpretive signs that guide visitors through the history and significance of the site. The trails offer a peaceful way to explore the area and understand the context of the Wright brothers' experiments.

What People Love About the Wright Brothers National Memorial

- Historical Significance: The memorial is situated at the exact location where aviation history was made. Visitors are moved by the sense of standing where the Wright brothers achieved the first powered flight, a milestone that changed the world.
- Educational Value: The exhibits and displays provide a thorough and engaging look at the Wright brothers' journey, from their early glider experiments to their ultimate success with powered flight. The detailed information and interactive elements make the learning experience enjoyable and informative.
- Inspiring Story: The story of the Wright brothers is one of innovation, perseverance, and triumph over adversity. Visitors find inspiration in their dedication and ingenuity, which are beautifully showcased throughout the memorial.
- Scenic Beauty: The location of the memorial, with its views of the Atlantic Ocean and surrounding landscape, adds to the experience. The site offers a serene and picturesque setting that enhances the reflective nature of the visit.
- Family-Friendly Atmosphere: The memorial is an excellent destination for families, with its interactive exhibits, open spaces, and educational programs. Children and adults alike

can enjoy learning about aviation history in a hands-on and engaging environment.

Tips for Visiting
- Plan Your Visit: Check the National Park Service website for the memorial's hours of operation, special events, and ranger-led programs. Planning ahead ensures you can take full advantage of all the site has to offer.
- Wear Comfortable Shoes: The park grounds and trails require some walking, so comfortable footwear is recommended.
- Bring a Camera: The scenic views and historic landmarks are worth capturing. Photography is allowed, so don't forget your camera or smartphone.
- Stay Hydrated and Protected: Bring water, sunscreen, and hats, especially during warmer months. There are few shaded areas, so it's important to stay hydrated and protected from the sun.
- Visit Nearby Attractions: The Outer Banks region offers additional attractions such as the nearby Jockey's Ridge State Park, where you can see the East Coast's tallest sand dunes and enjoy more outdoor activities.

The Wright Brothers National Memorial is more than just a tribute to the pioneers of flight; it's a place of inspiration and education that celebrates human ingenuity and the spirit of exploration. Whether you're an aviation enthusiast or simply curious about the history of flight, the memorial offers an enriching and memorable experience.

CHAPTER 7: FAMILY FRIENDLY ACTIVITIES

Family Fun at the Columbus Zoo and Aquarium

The Columbus Zoo and Aquarium is a top destination for families, offering a wide range of attractions and exhibits that provide both entertainment and education. Here's a guide to making the most of your visit, including key highlights, things to love, and safety tips:

Key Highlights

Animal Exhibits
- African Savanna: Encounter giraffes, zebras, and rhinos in a recreated African landscape.
- Polar Frontier: Watch polar bears swim and play in their expansive habitat.
- Asia Quest: Discover tigers, red pandas, and other fascinating animals from Asia.

Aquarium
- Manatee Coast: View manatees up close in this unique exhibit dedicated to these gentle giants.
- Discovery Reef: Explore a vibrant coral reef teeming with colorful fish and marine life.

Special Attractions
- Conservation Carousel: A beautifully crafted carousel featuring hand-carved animal figures.
- Train Rides: Enjoy a scenic train ride through the zoo's North America region.
- 4-D Theater: Experience movies with special effects like wind, water, and scents.

Things to Love

Interactive Experiences
- Animal Encounters Village: Get up close with small animals and learn about their care.
- Petting Zoo: Kids can interact with farm animals, including goats and sheep.

- Feeding Stations: Feed giraffes and stingrays for a hands-on experience.

Educational Programs
- Keeper Talks: Attend scheduled talks by zookeepers to learn more about the animals.
- Wild Encounters: Participate in behind-the-scenes tours and meet some of the zoo's animal ambassadors.

Family-Friendly Amenities
- Picnic Areas: Bring your own lunch and enjoy a picnic at one of the designated areas.
- Stroller and Wheelchair Rentals: Available for rent to make your visit more comfortable.
- Dining Options: Numerous cafes and food stands offer a variety of meals and snacks.

Safety Tips

Stay Hydrated
- Water Stations: Bring a refillable water bottle and take advantage of water refill stations throughout the zoo.

Sun Protection
- Sunscreen and Hats: Apply sunscreen regularly and wear hats to protect against sunburn.
- Shade Areas: Take breaks in shaded areas to avoid overexposure to the sun.

Child Safety
- Identification Bands: Use the zoo's free identification wristbands for children, which include your contact information in case of separation.
- Stay Together: Always keep an eye on your children and establish a meeting point in case anyone gets lost.

Respect the Animals
- Viewing Barriers: Stay behind barriers and never attempt to touch or feed animals unless in designated areas.
- Quiet Zones: Keep noise levels low around sensitive animal exhibits to avoid stressing the animals.

Health and Hygiene
- Hand Sanitizers: Use hand sanitizing stations frequently, especially after touching animals or using public facilities.
- Restroom Breaks: Take regular restroom breaks to keep everyone comfortable and clean.

The Columbus Zoo and Aquarium offers a fun and educational experience for the whole family. With its diverse animal exhibits, interactive attractions, and commitment to conservation, it's a place where both kids and adults can learn and play.

Rocking Out at the Rock and Roll Hall of Fame

The Rock and Roll Hall of Fame, located in Cleveland, Ohio, is a must-visit destination for music lovers. This iconic museum celebrates the legends and milestones of rock and roll, offering an immersive experience that brings the history of this influential genre to life. Here's a guide to making the most of your visit:

Key Highlights

Exhibits and Galleries
- The Hall of Fame: Explore the exhibits dedicated to the inductees, featuring artifacts, memorabilia, and personal items from some of the greatest rock and roll artists in history.
- The Legends of Rock: Dive into the stories of rock and roll icons through exhibits showcasing

their instruments, costumes, and personal belongings.
- The Beatles Exhibit: Discover the impact of The Beatles on music and culture with a collection of rare artifacts and interactive displays.

Interactive Experiences
- The Power of Rock Experience: An electrifying multi-sensory show that brings the power and passion of rock and roll to life.
- Jam Sessions: Participate in interactive exhibits where you can play instruments and create your own rock and roll tunes.

Temporary Exhibits
- Rotating Exhibits: The museum regularly hosts temporary exhibits that highlight different aspects of rock and roll, from specific artists and bands to broader cultural movements.

Things to Love

In-Depth History
- Comprehensive Coverage: The museum covers the entire history of rock and roll, from its roots in blues and gospel to its modern-day evolution.
- Rare Artifacts: See iconic artifacts up close, including handwritten lyrics, stage costumes, and legendary instruments.

Engaging Multimedia
- Documentaries and Films: Enjoy a variety of documentaries and films that tell the stories of rock and roll legends and pivotal moments in music history.
- Listening Stations: Listen to classic tracks and discover new favorites at the museum's many listening stations.

Family-Friendly Attractions
- Interactive Exhibits: Kids and adults alike can enjoy interactive exhibits that offer hands-on experiences with music and instruments.
- Gift Shop: Pick up rock and roll memorabilia and souvenirs to remember your visit.

Safety Tips

Plan Ahead
- Tickets: Purchase tickets online in advance to ensure entry and avoid long lines.
- Museum Map: Grab a museum map upon arrival to help navigate the exhibits and make the most of your visit.

Health and Safety
- Sanitization: Use hand sanitizing stations located throughout the museum, especially after interactive exhibits.
- Masks: Follow any current health guidelines regarding mask-wearing and social distancing.

Respect the Exhibits
- No Touching: Respect the museum's rules about not touching artifacts and exhibits to help preserve them for future visitors.
- Photography: Be mindful of photography rules; some exhibits may have restrictions on flash photography.

The Rock and Roll Hall of Fame offers a vibrant and educational experience for anyone with a passion for music. With its extensive exhibits, interactive experiences, and rich history, it's a place where the legacy of rock and roll comes to life.

Thrills and Spills at Cedar Point Amusement Park

Cedar Point Amusement Park, located in Sandusky, Ohio, is renowned for its thrilling rides and exciting attractions. Known as the "Roller Coaster Capital of the World," Cedar Point offers an unforgettable experience for thrill-seekers and families alike. Here's a guide to making the most of your visit:

Key Highlights

World-Class Roller Coasters
- Millennium Force: This iconic coaster is a must-ride, known for its incredible speed, height, and smooth ride.
- Steel Vengeance: The world's tallest, fastest, and longest hybrid coaster offers an exhilarating blend of steel and wood.
- Top Thrill Dragster: Experience a rapid launch and breathtaking heights on this record-breaking coaster.

Family-Friendly Attractions
- Planet Snoopy: A dedicated area for young children, featuring Peanuts-themed rides and attractions.
- Cedar Point Shores Waterpark: Cool off with a variety of water slides, wave pools, and lazy rivers.

Ohio Travel Guide 2025

Special Attractions
- Dinosaurs Alive!: An interactive walk-through attraction featuring life-sized animatronic dinosaurs.
- Live Entertainment: Enjoy shows and performances throughout the park, including music, dance, and comedy acts.

Things to Love

Thrilling Rides
- Variety of Coasters: With over 70 rides, including 18 world-class roller coasters, there's something for every thrill-seeker.
- Adrenaline-Pumping Experiences: The park's coasters and thrill rides provide heart-pounding excitement and unforgettable memories.

Family Fun
- Kid-Friendly Rides: Planet Snoopy and the Camp Snoopy area offer a variety of rides and attractions for younger guests.
- Waterpark Fun: Cedar Point Shores Waterpark provides a perfect way to beat the heat and enjoy water-based fun.

Beautiful Setting
- Lake Erie Views: The park is situated on a scenic peninsula, offering stunning views of Lake Erie.

- Beach Access: Enjoy a relaxing break on Cedar Point Beach, with its sandy shores and gentle waves.

Safety Tips

Stay Hydrated
- Water Stations: Bring a refillable water bottle and take advantage of water refill stations throughout the park.

Sun Protection
- Sunscreen and Hats: Apply sunscreen regularly and wear hats to protect against sunburn.
- Shade Areas: Take breaks in shaded areas to avoid overexposure to the sun.

Ride Safety
- Height Requirements: Check height requirements for each ride to ensure safety and compliance.
- Follow Instructions: Always follow the ride operators' instructions and safety guidelines.

Child Safety
- Identification Bands: Use the park's free identification wristbands for children, which include your contact information in case of separation.

- Stay Together: Always keep an eye on your children and establish a meeting point in case anyone gets lost.

Health and Hygiene
- Hand Sanitizers: Use hand sanitizing stations frequently, especially after touching ride safety bars or using public facilities.
- Restroom Breaks: Take regular restroom breaks to keep everyone comfortable and clean.

Cedar Point Amusement Park offers an exciting and enjoyable experience for visitors of all ages. With its world-class roller coasters, family-friendly attractions, and beautiful setting, it's a destination that promises thrills and spills for everyone.

Hands-on Learning at the Imagination Station

The Imagination Station, located in Toledo, Ohio, is an interactive science center that offers hands-on learning experiences for visitors of all ages. With its engaging exhibits and educational programs, the Imagination Station provides a fun and immersive environment where curiosity and creativity thrive. Here's a guide to making the most of your visit:

Key Highlights

Interactive Exhibits
- Energy Factory: Explore the science of energy through interactive exhibits that demonstrate principles of electricity, magnetism, and renewable energy.
- Water Works: Discover the properties of water with exhibits that allow you to experiment with currents, waves, and water pressure.
- Gravity Room: Experience the effects of gravity and learn about the forces that shape our world.

Live Demonstrations
- Science Shows: Enjoy live science demonstrations that cover a variety of topics,

from chemistry experiments to physics demonstrations.
- Dissection Labs: Participate in hands-on dissection labs to learn about anatomy and biology.

Kid-Friendly Zones
- Little Kidspace: Designed for children ages 5 and under, this area offers age-appropriate exhibits that encourage exploration and play.
- Mini Explorers Club: Engage in themed activities and experiments designed specifically for young children.

Things to Love

Hands-On Learning
- Interactive Exhibits: The Imagination Station's hands-on exhibits make learning science fun and engaging for visitors of all ages.
- Educational Programs: From workshops and camps to school programs and field trips, the center offers a variety of educational opportunities.

Family-Friendly Environment
- Inclusive Spaces: The center provides exhibits and activities that cater to different age groups and learning styles.

- Safe and Welcoming: The Imagination Station is designed to be a safe and welcoming space for families to explore and learn together.

Special Events
- Themed Days: Participate in special themed days that focus on specific scientific topics, such as space exploration or environmental science.
- Guest Speakers: Attend talks and presentations by guest scientists and educators.

Safety Tips

Supervise Children
- Stay Together: Keep an eye on your children and make sure they stay within sight while exploring the exhibits.
- Hands-On Guidance: Encourage your children to explore and experiment, but provide guidance to ensure they use the exhibits safely.

Health and Hygiene
- Hand Sanitizers: Use hand sanitizing stations frequently, especially after touching exhibits and before eating.
- Restroom Breaks: Take regular restroom breaks to keep everyone comfortable and clean.

Respect the Exhibits
- Follow Rules: Respect the center's rules about using the exhibits properly to ensure they remain in good condition for all visitors.
- No Running: Remind children to walk and not run inside the center to avoid accidents.

The Imagination Station offers a dynamic and enriching experience that sparks curiosity and fosters a love of learning. With its wide range of interactive exhibits, educational programs, and family-friendly environment, it's a place where science comes to life in exciting and memorable ways.

Adventures at Kings Island Amusement Park

Kings Island Amusement Park, located in Mason, Ohio, is one of the premier amusement parks in the Midwest. Known for its world-class roller coasters, family-friendly attractions, and vibrant entertainment, Kings Island offers an unforgettable experience for thrill-seekers and families alike. Here's a guide to making the most of your visit:

Key Highlights

Thrilling Roller Coasters
- Orion: One of the park's newest and tallest roller coasters, Orion offers a high-speed, out-of-this-world experience.
- Diamondback: This steel coaster features a series of drops and twists that provide non-stop excitement.
- The Beast: Known as the longest wooden roller coaster in the world, The Beast offers an exhilarating ride through the woods.

Family-Friendly Attractions
- Planet Snoopy: A dedicated area for young children with Peanuts-themed rides and attractions.
- Grand Carousel: A classic carousel ride that's perfect for all ages.
- Kings Mills Antique Autos: Take a leisurely drive in vintage-style cars around a scenic track.

Water Park Fun
- Soak City: The park's water park offers a variety of slides, wave pools, and lazy rivers, perfect for cooling off on a hot day.

Live Entertainment
- Shows and Performances: Enjoy live shows and musical performances throughout the park,

featuring everything from stunt shows to musical acts.

Things to Love

Variety of Rides
- Wide Range of Coasters: With over 100 rides and attractions, including 14 roller coasters, there's something for every thrill level.
- Water Park: Soak City provides a great way to beat the heat with its water attractions.

Family Fun
- Kid-Friendly Areas: Planet Snoopy and other family attractions ensure that younger visitors have plenty of fun options.
- Interactive Experiences: Meet and greet opportunities with Peanuts characters and other interactive attractions.

Beautiful Setting
- Park Scenery: The park is beautifully landscaped, providing a pleasant environment for strolling and relaxing.
- Seasonal Events: Seasonal decorations and events add to the charm and excitement.

Safety Tips

Stay Hydrated
- Water Stations: Bring a refillable water bottle and take advantage of water refill stations throughout the park.

Sun Protection
- Sunscreen and Hats: Apply sunscreen regularly and wear hats to protect against sunburn.
- Shade Areas: Take breaks in shaded areas to avoid overexposure to the sun.

Ride Safety
- Height Requirements: Check height requirements for each ride to ensure safety and compliance.
- Follow Instructions: Always follow the ride operators' instructions and safety guidelines.

Child Safety
- Identification Bands: Use the park's free identification wristbands for children, which include your contact information in case of separation.
- Stay Together: Always keep an eye on your children and establish a meeting point in case anyone gets lost.

Health and Hygiene
- Hand Sanitizers: Use hand sanitizing stations frequently, especially after touching ride safety bars or using public facilities.
- Restroom Breaks: Take regular restroom breaks to keep everyone comfortable and clean.

Kings Island Amusement Park offers an exciting and memorable experience for visitors of all ages. With its world-class roller coasters, family-friendly attractions, and beautiful setting, it's a destination that promises thrills and fun for everyone.

CHAPTER 8: DINING AND CUISINE

Must-Try Ohio Foods

Ohio is a treasure trove of culinary delights, offering a diverse range of flavors influenced by its rich cultural heritage. Here are some must-try Ohio foods and the best places to enjoy them:

Cincinnati Chili: This unique chili is made with Mediterranean-inspired spices, including cinnamon and chocolate. It's typically served over spaghetti with shredded cheddar and onions. Try it at Skyline Chili or Gold Star Chili in Cincinnati.

Buckeyes: Named after Ohio's state tree, these candies are made from peanut butter balls dipped in chocolate, leaving a small portion uncovered. You can find them at local specialty food stores or Amish markets throughout the state.

Pierogies: These Eastern European dumplings are filled with potatoes, cheese, or sauerkraut. Sokolowski's

University Inn in Cleveland is a popular spot to enjoy authentic pierogies.

The Thurmanator: This massive burger from Thurman Cafe in Columbus includes two 12-ounce beef patties, bacon, ham, and multiple types of cheese. Visit Thurman Cafe to take on this challenge.

Barberton Chicken: Originating from Barberton, Ohio, this Serbian-style fried chicken is served with coleslaw and hot rice. DeVore's Hopocan Gardens and White House Chicken in Barberton are great places to try this dish.

Goetta: A German-inspired sausage made with oats. Glier's Goettafest in Cincinnati celebrates this unique sausage, and you can find it in many local grocery stores.

Jacky's Depot Ice Cream: Known for its homemade, super-premium ice cream, Jacky's Depot in Maumee offers unique flavors and gourmet ice cream cookie sandwiches. Stop by Jacky's Depot for a sweet treat.

Shoofly Pie: This traditional Amish pie has a molasses filling and a crumbly topping. Golden Lamb in Lebanon serves this classic dessert.

Campus Pollyeyes Stuffed Breadsticks: Located near Bowling Green State University, this cozy spot is famous for its stuffed breadsticks filled with cheese and various toppings. Visit Campus Pollyeyes for a filling meal

Schmidt's Sausage Haus Bahama Mama: This German Village landmark in Columbus is known for its hickory-smoked beef and pork sausages and jumbo cream puffs. Try the Bahama Mama sausage and cream puffs at Schmidt's Sausage Haus.

Ohio's culinary scene is a delightful mix of traditional and unique dishes that reflect its diverse cultural influences. Whether you're a fan of hearty meals or sweet treats, there's something for everyone to enjoy in the Buckeye State.

Best Restaurants in Ohio

Ohio boasts a vibrant culinary scene with a diverse range of dining options. From fine dining establishments to cozy diners, there's something for every palate. Here are some of the best restaurants in Ohio that you should definitely try:

Mitas (Cincinnati): This tapas bar offers a delightful array of Spanish-inspired dishes, including paella, salt-cured meats, and goat cheese-stuffed peppers. Chef Jose Salazar's creations are a testament to his culinary prowess.

Forage Public House (Lakewood): Known for its farm-to-table approach, Forage Public House features a colorful and creative menu. Don't miss their grilled Amish chicken and seasonal dishes made from local ingredients.

Guarino's Ristorante (Cleveland): Established in 1918, this Italian restaurant in Cleveland's Little Italy is famous for its lasagna and other Old Country recipes. It's a perfect spot for a romantic dinner.

The Spot (Sidney): This classic diner offers a nostalgic dining experience with its cheeseburgers and old-fashioned charm. It's a great place for a road trip stop.

Mrs. Yoder's Kitchen (Amish Country): Enjoy authentic Amish cuisine at this family-friendly restaurant. Their homemade meals and welcoming atmosphere make it a must-visit.

Mike's Place (Kent): This eclectic restaurant features a mix of classic and inventive dishes, served in a whimsical setting with hand-painted signs and unique decor. Their triple-decker Reuben is a crowd favorite.

Boca (Cincinnati): For a fine dining experience, Boca offers a classy and luxurious atmosphere with a menu that features innovative dishes and top-quality ingredients.

Southside Diner (Mount Vernon): This 50s and 60s-style diner serves homemade meals and unbeatable desserts. The turkey boat and roast beef sandwich are popular choices among guests.

Red Oak Pub and Restaurant (Newark): Known for its delicious burgers and steak fries, Red Oak Pub is a great spot to catch a game while enjoying a hearty meal.

Opa Grill & Tavern (Delaware): This Mediterranean grill offers a variety of spreads, dips, and gyros made from scratch. The friendly staff and great food make it a local favorite.

Ohio's culinary landscape is rich and varied, offering something for everyone. Whether you're in the mood for a casual meal or a fine dining experience, these restaurants are sure to satisfy your cravings.

Food Festivals and Events

Ohio is home to a vibrant food scene, and its festivals and events are a testament to the state's rich culinary culture. Here are some of the top food festivals and events in Ohio that you won't want to miss:

Taste of Cincinnati: Held annually in May, this is the nation's longest-running culinary arts festival. It features over 50 local restaurants and food trucks serving their signature dishes, along with live entertainment and craft beer stations.

Cleveland International Film Festival (CIFF) Film and Food Fest: This festival combines the love of cinema with gourmet food, offering a unique experience for film and food enthusiasts. Held in March, it features food trucks, local chefs, and a variety of international cuisines.

Cincinnati Chili Fest: Celebrate the unique flavors of Cincinnati chili in January at Findley Market. This festival showcases the best chili recipes from local restaurants and vendors.

Ohio Wine & Craft Beer Festival: Held in various locations across the state, this festival celebrates Ohio's finest wines and craft beers. It's a great opportunity to sample a wide range of beverages from local breweries and wineries.

Jazz & Rib Fest: Taking place in July in Columbus, this festival offers a mouthwatering selection of ribs from award-winning barbecue teams, along with live jazz performances.

Ohio Swiss Festival: Held in Sugarcreek in September, this festival celebrates the area's Swiss heritage with parades, a 5K run, and an abundance of Swiss cuisine, including the famous Swiss cheese.

Bucyrus Bratwurst Festival: In August, Bucyrus hosts this festival featuring the best bratwursts in the state. It's a fun-filled event with plenty of food, music, and family activities.

Banana Split Festival: Celebrate the creation of the banana split in Wilmington in June. This festival offers a variety of banana split-themed treats and activities for all ages.

A World A'Fair: Held in Dayton in May, this international festival showcases the ethnic backgrounds and cultures of the Miami Valley with food booths from over 30 countries.

Oktoberfest Zinzinnati: One of the largest Oktoberfest celebrations in the United States, this event takes place in Cincinnati in September and features German food, beer, music, and traditional Bavarian costumes.

These festivals and events offer a fantastic way to experience Ohio's diverse culinary offerings while enjoying the vibrant atmosphere and community spirit. Whether you're a foodie, a beer lover, or just looking for a fun outing, there's something for everyone to enjoy in Ohio.

Farmers' Markets

Ohio is home to a wealth of farmers' markets where visitors can find fresh produce, handcrafted goods, and a vibrant community atmosphere. These markets provide a great way to support local farmers, artisans, and small businesses while enjoying high-quality, locally sourced products. Here are some of the best farmers' markets in Ohio:

North Market (Columbus): Located in the Short North Arts District, North Market is a bustling public market that offers a variety of fresh produce, meats, cheeses, baked goods, and prepared foods. It's a one-stop-shop for local specialties and artisanal products.

West Side Market (Cleveland): Established in 1912, this historic market is a Cleveland institution. With over 100 vendors, it offers a diverse selection of fresh produce, meats, seafood, dairy products, baked goods, and ethnic foods. The market's beautiful architecture adds to its charm.

Findlay Market (Cincinnati): Ohio's oldest continuously operated public market, Findlay Market is located in the historic Over-the-Rhine neighborhood. It features a wide range of local and international foods, as well as handmade crafts and flowers. The market hosts seasonal farmers' markets and events throughout the year.

Worthington Farmers Market (Worthington): This popular market operates year-round, offering an impressive array of fresh produce, meats, cheeses, baked goods, and plants. The summer market is held outdoors in historic downtown Worthington, while the winter market moves indoors.

Athens Farmers Market (Athens): Known for its community atmosphere and diverse selection, the Athens Farmers Market offers fresh produce, meats, dairy products, baked goods, and crafts. It operates year-round and is a favorite among locals and students from Ohio University.

Shaker Square Farmers Market (Cleveland): Located in the historic Shaker Square, this market features a variety of locally grown produce, meats, cheeses, baked goods, and artisanal products. It operates from April through December and offers a lively community experience.

Toledo Farmers Market (Toledo): This market has been serving the community for over 180 years and offers a wide range of fresh produce, flowers, plants, baked goods, and crafts. The market operates year-round, with both indoor and outdoor vendors.

Yellow Springs Farmers Market (Yellow Springs): This charming market is held every Saturday from May to November and features fresh produce, meats, cheeses, baked goods, flowers, and handmade crafts. It's a great place to experience the local flavor and community spirit of Yellow Springs.

Medina Farmers Market (Medina): Located on Medina's historic square, this market offers a variety of fresh produce, meats, cheeses, baked goods, and handcrafted items. The market runs from May to October and includes live music and family-friendly activities.

Chagrin Falls Farmers Market (Chagrin Falls): This market takes place in the heart of Chagrin Falls, offering fresh produce, meats, cheeses, baked goods, and handmade crafts. It operates from June to October and provides a scenic and enjoyable shopping experience.

Farmers' markets in Ohio offer more than just fresh produce; they provide a vibrant community space where visitors can connect with local farmers, artisans, and fellow food enthusiasts. Whether you're looking for seasonal fruits and vegetables, artisanal cheeses, or handcrafted goods, Ohio's farmers' markets have something for everyone.

Ohio Travel Guide 2025

CHAPTER 9: ACCOMMODATIONS

Luxury Hotels

Ohio offers a variety of luxury hotels that provide exceptional service, stunning architecture, and top-notch amenities. Whether you're visiting for business or leisure, these hotels ensure a memorable stay with their unique charm and high standards. Here are the top three luxury hotels in Ohio, along with their key highlights and what people love about them:

The Lytle Park Hotel, Autograph Collection (Cincinnati)

Key Highlights
- Rooftop Restaurant: Offers stunning views of the city and a sophisticated dining experience.

Ohio Travel Guide 2025

- Fitness Center: Well-equipped for a variety of workouts.
- Elegant Design: Beautiful architecture and stylish interiors.

What People Love
- Beautiful Architecture: Guests appreciate the blend of historic charm and modern luxury.
- Convenient Location: Situated in the heart of Cincinnati, making it easy to explore the city.
- Rooftop Dining: The rooftop restaurant is a highlight, offering great food and views.

Hotel LeVeque, Autograph Collection (Columbus)

Key Highlights
- Historic Skyscraper: Located in a beautifully restored building with art deco elements.

- On-site Bar: Offers a relaxing space to unwind.
- Fitness Center: Equipped with modern amenities for guests.

What People Love
- Central Location: In the heart of Columbus, close to major attractions and dining options.
- Art Deco Murals: The unique and historic decor is a favorite among guests.
- Cozy Rooms: The rooms are described as comfortable and well-appointed.

Hilton Cleveland Downtown (Cleveland)

Key Highlights
- Stunning Views: Overlooks Lake Erie and the Cleveland skyline.
- Modern Design: Features contemporary decor and spacious rooms.

- On-site Restaurant and Bar: Offers exceptional dining and beverage options.

What People Love
- Scenic Views: Guests love the breathtaking views of Lake Erie and the city.
- Vibrant Location: Situated in downtown Cleveland, close to attractions like the Rock & Roll Hall of Fame.
- Spacious and Clean Rooms: The rooms are praised for their comfort and cleanliness.

These luxury hotels offer a blend of exceptional service, beautiful design, and prime locations, ensuring a memorable stay for any traveler.

Mid-Range Hotels

Ohio offers a variety of mid-range hotels that provide comfort, convenience, and excellent value for travelers. Whether you're visiting for business or leisure, these hotels offer a pleasant and enjoyable stay without breaking the bank. Here are some of the best mid-range hotels in Ohio, along with their key highlights and what people love about them:

Drury Inn & Suites Columbus Convention Center (Columbus)

Key Highlights
- Location: Conveniently located near the Greater Columbus Convention Center and downtown attractions.
- Amenities: Offers complimentary hot breakfast, evening receptions with snacks and drinks, indoor pool, and fitness center.
- Room Comfort: Spacious and clean rooms equipped with modern amenities.

What People Love
- Value for Money: Guests appreciate the complimentary breakfast and evening receptions, adding great value to their stay.

- Friendly Staff: The hotel staff is known for their helpfulness and friendly service.
- Central Location: Proximity to major attractions and dining options in downtown Columbus.

Hampton Inn & Suites Toledo-Perrysburg (Rossford)

Key Highlights
- Location: Situated near Perrysburg, offering easy access to both Toledo and local attractions.
- Amenities: Provides free hot breakfast, indoor pool, fitness center, and business facilities.
- Room Comfort: Clean and comfortable rooms with modern furnishings.

What People Love
- Great Breakfast: Guests enjoy the variety and quality of the complimentary breakfast.
- Convenient Location: Easy access to highways, making it convenient for travelers.
- Cleanliness and Comfort: High marks for clean and comfortable accommodations.

Courtyard by Marriott Cleveland University Circle (Cleveland)

Key Highlights
- Location: Located in the University Circle area, close to museums, hospitals, and Case Western Reserve University.
- Amenities: Features an on-site bistro, fitness center, indoor pool, and business center.

- Room Comfort: Modern and spacious rooms with ergonomic workspaces.

What People Love
- Proximity to Attractions: Close to the Cleveland Museum of Art, Cleveland Botanical Garden, and other cultural institutions.
- Friendly and Professional Staff: Guests appreciate the welcoming and efficient service.
- Comfortable Rooms: Modern amenities and comfortable beds contribute to a pleasant stay.

These mid-range hotels in Ohio offer a comfortable and affordable stay with a range of amenities and excellent service. Whether you're traveling for business or leisure, these hotels provide great value and a pleasant experience.

Budget-Friendly Options

Traveling on a budget doesn't mean you have to sacrifice comfort. Ohio offers a wide range of budget-friendly hotels that provide excellent amenities and service at an affordable price. Here are some of the best budget-friendly hotels in Ohio, along with their key highlights and what people love about them:

Red Roof PLUS+ Columbus Downtown-Convention Center (Columbus)

Key Highlights
- Location: Conveniently located near the Greater Columbus Convention Center and downtown attractions.
- Amenities: Offers free Wi-Fi, complimentary coffee, and pet-friendly accommodations.
- Room Comfort: Clean and modern rooms with comfortable bedding.

What People Love
- Great Value: Guests appreciate the affordable rates and convenient location.
- Pet-Friendly: The hotel is welcoming to pets, making it a great choice for travelers with furry friends.

- Friendly Staff: The staff is known for their helpful and friendly service.

Motel 6 Cleveland Middleburg Heights (Cleveland)

Key Highlights
- Location: Located near the Cleveland Hopkins International Airport and major highways.
- Amenities: Offers free Wi-Fi, complimentary morning coffee, and an outdoor pool.
- Room Comfort: Simple and clean rooms with essential amenities.

What People Love
- Budget-Friendly Rates: Guests find the rates to be very reasonable, especially for the location.

- Convenient Location: Proximity to the airport and highways makes it easy to get around.
- Cleanliness: The rooms are praised for being clean and well-maintained.

Days Inn by Wyndham Cincinnati East (Cincinnati)

Key Highlights
- Location: Situated near I-275, providing easy access to downtown Cincinnati and local attractions.
- Amenities: Offers free continental breakfast, Wi-Fi, and an outdoor pool.
- Room Comfort: Comfortable rooms with basic amenities and modern furnishings.

What People Love
- Complimentary Breakfast: The free breakfast adds value to the stay.
- Affordable Rates: Guests appreciate the cost-effective pricing.
- Friendly Service: The staff is noted for their welcoming and helpful attitude.

These budget-friendly hotels in Ohio provide comfortable accommodations and essential amenities at an affordable price, ensuring a pleasant stay without straining your budget. Whether you're visiting for business or leisure, these hotels offer great value and convenience.

Unique Stays

Ohio offers a variety of unique and unconventional accommodations that provide a truly memorable experience. Whether you're seeking a rustic retreat, a historic landmark, or an unusual setting, these unique stays are sure to make your visit to Ohio unforgettable. Here are some of the best unique stays in Ohio:

The Mohicans Treehouse Resort (Glenmont)

Key Highlights
- Treehouses and Cabins: Stay in beautifully designed treehouses or cozy cabins nestled in the woods.
- Nature Immersion: Surrounded by the lush forest, offering a peaceful and serene environment.
- Eco-Friendly: Focus on sustainability with eco-friendly practices.

What People Love
- Magical Atmosphere: Guests love the enchanting feeling of staying in a treehouse.
- Seclusion and Privacy: The remote location provides a perfect getaway from the hustle and bustle.

- Unique Experience: The combination of rustic charm and modern amenities creates a one-of-a-kind stay.

The Inn at Honey Run (Millersburg)

Key Highlights
- Earth-Sheltered Rooms: Unique hillside rooms that blend seamlessly with the natural landscape.
- Scenic Trails: Miles of hiking trails through beautiful woodland and meadows.
- Fine Dining: The on-site Tarragon restaurant offers gourmet meals with a focus on local ingredients.

What People Love
- Peaceful Retreat: Guests appreciate the tranquility and natural beauty of the surroundings.
- Unique Accommodations: The earth-sheltered rooms provide a distinctive and cozy experience.
- Excellent Dining: The gourmet meals at Tarragon receive high praise.

Ravenwood Castle (New Plymouth)

Key Highlights
- Medieval-Themed Rooms: Stay in a castle, cottages, or cabins with medieval décor and ambiance.
- Scenic Location: Located in the picturesque Hocking Hills region.

- On-Site Tavern: The Great Hall offers hearty meals and a selection of craft beers.

What People Love
- Fairytale Setting: Guests love the immersive experience of staying in a medieval-themed castle.
- Adventure Opportunities: Proximity to Hocking Hills State Park for hiking, zip-lining, and exploring.
- Friendly Atmosphere: The warm and welcoming staff enhance the overall experience.

What People Love
- Novelty and Fun: Guests enjoy the fun and quirky experience of staying in a train caboose.
- Comfortable Accommodations: Despite its small size, the caboose is well-equipped and comfortable.
- Beautiful Location: Proximity to hiking trails and natural attractions in Hocking Hills.

These unique stays in Ohio offer a range of experiences, from rustic treehouses to historic inns, ensuring a memorable and special getaway. Whether you're looking for adventure, relaxation, or a step back in time, these accommodations provide something truly unique.

CHAPTER 10: TRANSPORTATION AND GETTING AROUND

Public Transportation Options

Ohio offers a variety of public transportation options that cater to the needs of commuters, tourists, and residents alike. These options provide a convenient, cost-effective, and environmentally friendly way to get around the state. Here are some key highlights, types of public transportation, and what people love about them:

Types of Public Transportation in Ohio
- Bus Services: Most major cities in Ohio, including Cleveland, Cincinnati, and Columbus, have extensive bus networks that cover both urban and suburban areas.
- Light Rail and Streetcars: Cities like Cleveland have light rail systems, while Cincinnati offers a streetcar service.
- Ferry Services: Some areas, particularly those near water bodies, offer ferry services for both commuters and tourists.
- Ride-Sharing and Bike-Sharing: Services like Uber, Lyft, and local bike-sharing programs provide flexible transportation options.
- Specialized Transit for Seniors and People with Disabilities: Many transit systems offer specialized services to ensure accessibility for all residents.

Advantages of Public Transportation in Ohio
- Cost-Effective: Public transportation is generally more affordable than owning and maintaining a car, especially in urban areas.
- Environmental Benefits: Using public transportation reduces the number of vehicles on the road, which helps lower greenhouse gas emissions and traffic congestion.
- Convenience: Public transit systems are designed to connect major points of interest, making it easy to travel without the hassle of parking and navigating traffic.
- Accessibility: Many transit systems offer services tailored to seniors and people with disabilities, ensuring that everyone can travel safely and comfortably.

Key Highlights
- Extensive Coverage: Ohio's public transportation systems cover a wide range of areas, from bustling city centers to rural communities.
- Modern Amenities: Many transit systems offer free Wi-Fi, real-time tracking, and mobile ticketing options for added convenience.
- Economic Impact: Public transportation supports local economies by providing reliable access to jobs, education, and healthcare.

What People Love About Public Transportation in Ohio

- Reliability: Riders appreciate the punctuality and consistency of public transit services, which helps them plan their schedules effectively.
- Safety: Public transportation is considered a safe mode of travel, with well-maintained vehicles and trained staff.
- Community Connection: Using public transit allows people to interact with fellow residents, fostering a sense of community and shared experience.
- Ease of Use: With user-friendly apps and websites, planning and using public transportation has become more straightforward and efficient.

Public transportation in Ohio offers a range of options that cater to diverse needs and preferences, making it a practical and enjoyable way to travel around the state. Whether you're commuting to work, exploring new places, or simply getting around town, Ohio's public transit systems provide a reliable and accessible solution.

Car Rentals and Ridesharing

Ohio offers a range of transportation options that cater to different needs and preferences, including car rentals and ridesharing services. These options provide flexibility and convenience for travelers, whether you're visiting for business or leisure. Here's an overview of car rentals and ridesharing services in Ohio, along with their advantages, key highlights, and what people love about them:

Car Rentals

Car rentals are an excellent option for those who prefer the freedom to explore at their own pace. Ohio has a variety of car rental companies that offer a wide range of vehicles to suit different needs.

Key Highlights

- Wide Range of Choices: From economy cars to luxury vehicles and SUVs, car rental companies offer a diverse selection of vehicles.
- Convenient Locations: Rental offices are available at major airports, city centers, and suburban areas, making it easy to pick up and drop off vehicles.
- Flexible Rental Periods: Rent a car for a day, a week, or even longer, depending on your travel needs.
- Additional Services: Many companies offer add-ons such as GPS navigation, child seats, and roadside assistance for added convenience.

What People Love

- Freedom and Flexibility: Renting a car provides the freedom to explore Ohio's attractions, cities, and scenic routes at your own pace.

- Comfort and Privacy: Enjoy the comfort and privacy of your own vehicle, especially for longer trips.
- Cost-Effective for Groups: Car rentals can be a cost-effective option for families or groups traveling together.

Ridesharing Services

Ridesharing services like Uber and Lyft are popular choices for quick, convenient, and affordable transportation within cities and suburbs.

Key Highlights
- On-Demand Service: Request a ride with just a few taps on your smartphone, and a driver will arrive within minutes.
- Cashless Transactions: Payment is handled through the app, making the process smooth and cashless.
- Variety of Ride Options: Choose from a range of ride options, including standard rides, luxury vehicles, and carpooling options like UberPOOL or Lyft Line.
- Safety Features: Both Uber and Lyft offer safety features such as driver ratings, trip tracking, and the ability to share your ride status with friends and family.

What People Love
- Convenience: Ridesharing services are available 24/7, making it easy to get around at any time of day or night.
- Affordability: Ridesharing can be a cost-effective alternative to taxis, especially for short trips.
- Ease of Use: The user-friendly apps make it simple to request a ride, track your driver, and pay for the service.
- Safety and Reliability: Passengers appreciate the safety features and the reliability of ridesharing services.

Advantages of Car Rentals and Ridesharing
- Accessibility: Both car rentals and ridesharing services are widely available across Ohio, ensuring you can find transportation options wherever you are.
- Flexibility: Choose the option that best fits your travel needs, whether you prefer the independence of a rental car or the convenience of ridesharing.
- Cost-Effective: Depending on your travel plans, both options can offer cost-effective solutions for getting around.

Ohio's car rental and ridesharing options provide travelers with the flexibility and convenience needed to explore the state comfortably. Whether you're driving along scenic routes, heading to a business meeting, or exploring city attractions, these transportation options ensure you can get where you need to go with ease.

Bike Shares and Scooters

Ohio's cities have embraced bike-sharing and scooter-sharing programs as convenient, eco-friendly transportation options. These services offer residents and visitors an easy way to navigate urban areas while reducing traffic congestion and carbon emissions. Here's an overview of bike shares and scooters in Ohio, along with their key highlights, advantages, and what people love about them:

Types of Bike Shares and Scooters in Ohio

Bike Sharing Programs
- CoGo Bike Share (Columbus): CoGo offers a network of bikes available for short-term rental across Columbus. The system includes both traditional pedal bikes and electric-assist bikes, making it accessible to riders of various fitness levels.
- Lime Bikes (Cleveland and other cities): Lime provides dockless bike-sharing services, allowing users to find and unlock bikes through a mobile app. These bikes are available in multiple Ohio cities.
- Link Dayton Bike Share (Dayton): Link offers both pedal bikes and electric-assist bikes for short-term rentals, with stations located

throughout downtown Dayton and surrounding neighborhoods.

Scooter Sharing Programs
- Bird and Lime Scooters (Multiple Cities): Bird and Lime offer electric scooters that can be rented and unlocked via mobile apps. These scooters are available in cities like Columbus, Cleveland, Cincinnati, and more.
- Spin Scooters (Cleveland): Spin provides electric scooters for short-term rentals, offering a convenient way to travel around the city.

Advantages of Bike Shares and Scooters
- Eco-Friendly: Both bike shares and scooters produce zero emissions, making them a sustainable choice for urban transportation.
- Convenient: These services are typically available 24/7, allowing users to pick up and drop off bikes or scooters at any time.
- Affordable: Bike and scooter rentals are generally affordable, with pay-as-you-go options and membership plans for frequent users.
- Reduces Traffic Congestion: By providing an alternative to cars, bike shares and scooters help reduce traffic congestion and improve urban mobility.

Key Highlights
- Accessibility: Many bike and scooter-sharing programs are designed to be easily accessible,

with numerous pick-up and drop-off locations throughout the cities.
- Technology Integration: Users can quickly locate, rent, and unlock bikes or scooters using mobile apps, making the process seamless and user-friendly.
- Health Benefits: Biking, in particular, offers physical health benefits, promoting exercise and an active lifestyle.

What People Love About Bike Shares and Scooters

- Flexibility: The ability to pick up a bike or scooter at one location and drop it off at another provides flexibility for users' travel plans.
- Ease of Use: The integration with mobile apps makes renting and using bikes and scooters simple and efficient.
- Fun and Enjoyable: Riding a bike or scooter can be a fun and enjoyable way to explore the city, offering a unique perspective compared to traditional modes of transportation.
- Cost-Effective Transportation: Users appreciate the affordability of bike shares and scooters, making them an economical choice for short trips and commuting.

Safety Tips

- Wear a Helmet: Always wear a helmet to protect yourself in case of falls or accidents.

- Follow Traffic Rules: Obey all traffic signals and signs, and ride in designated bike lanes whenever possible.
- Be Aware of Your Surroundings: Stay alert and watch out for pedestrians, vehicles, and other obstacles.
- Park Responsibly: When finished, park bikes and scooters in designated areas to avoid obstructing sidewalks and pathways.

Ohio's bike-sharing and scooter-sharing programs offer a convenient, eco-friendly, and fun way to get around urban areas. Whether you're commuting to work, running errands, or exploring the city, these services provide a flexible and enjoyable transportation option.

Navigating Ohio

Navigating Ohio is made easy with a variety of transportation options and resources that cater to different travel needs. Whether you're exploring vibrant cities, scenic countryside, or charming small towns, here's a comprehensive guide to help you get around Ohio smoothly and efficiently:

Public Transportation

Ohio's major cities offer extensive public transportation networks, including buses, light rail, and streetcars.
- Cleveland: The Greater Cleveland Regional Transit Authority (RTA) operates buses, a light

rail system, and the HealthLine BRT, which connects downtown with University Circle.
- Columbus: The Central Ohio Transit Authority (COTA) provides comprehensive bus services throughout the city and its suburbs.
- Cincinnati: The Southwest Ohio Regional Transit Authority (SORTA) operates Metro buses and the Cincinnati Bell Connector streetcar in downtown Cincinnati.
- Dayton: The Greater Dayton Regional Transit Authority (RTA) offers bus services and the historic electric trolley buses.

Highways and Roads

Ohio has a well-maintained network of highways and roads that make driving a convenient option for exploring the state.
- Interstate Highways: Major interstates like I-70, I-71, I-75, and I-80/I-90 (Ohio Turnpike) connect Ohio's cities and regions.
- State Routes: Ohio's state route system provides access to scenic byways, rural areas, and smaller towns.
- Scenic Byways: Take a leisurely drive along Ohio's scenic byways, such as the Ohio River Scenic Byway, Amish Country Byway, and Lake Erie Coastal Trail, to experience the state's natural beauty.

Car Rentals

Car rentals offer flexibility and convenience for those who prefer to travel at their own pace.

- Availability: Car rental services are available at major airports, city centers, and suburban locations. Companies like Enterprise, Hertz, Avis, and Budget provide a wide range of vehicles.
- Booking: Online booking and mobile apps make it easy to reserve a car in advance.

Ridesharing and Taxis

For quick and hassle-free transportation within cities, ridesharing and taxi services are widely available.

- Ridesharing: Services like Uber and Lyft operate in Ohio's major cities, offering on-demand rides with the convenience of cashless transactions.
- Taxis: Traditional taxi services are also available, particularly in larger cities and at transportation hubs.

Bike Shares and Scooters

Eco-friendly and fun, bike shares and scooters provide a great way to explore urban areas.

- Bike Sharing: Programs like CoGo Bike Share (Columbus), Link Dayton Bike Share, and Lime Bikes (various cities) offer short-term rentals with easy pickup and drop-off options.
- Scooters: Electric scooters from companies like Bird, Lime, and Spin are available in cities like Columbus, Cleveland, and Cincinnati. Rent and

unlock them via mobile apps for convenient travel.

Navigational Tools

To make navigation even easier, use these tools and resources:
- GPS Navigation: Apps like Google Maps, Waze, and Apple Maps provide real-time directions, traffic updates, and route planning.
- Transit Apps: Many public transit systems offer mobile apps with schedules, route maps, and real-time tracking. COTA, RTA, and SORTA all have dedicated apps.
- Travel Guides: Websites and apps like TripAdvisor and Yelp offer reviews, recommendations, and information on local attractions, restaurants, and more.

What People Love About Navigating Ohio

- Ease of Travel: The state's well-connected transportation network makes it easy to get around, whether by car, public transit, or other means.
- Scenic Drives: Ohio's scenic byways and countryside roads offer beautiful landscapes and a relaxing travel experience.
- Convenient Tools: Modern navigation tools and apps enhance the travel experience by providing real-time information and easy route planning.
- Diverse Options: The variety of transportation options ensures that travelers can choose the

best mode of transport to suit their needs and preferences.

Navigating Ohio is straightforward and enjoyable, thanks to the state's extensive transportation infrastructure and modern navigational tools. Whether you're commuting within a city, embarking on a road trip, or exploring new destinations, Ohio's travel options ensure a smooth and pleasant journey.

CHAPTER 11: LOCAL FESTIVALS AND EVENTS

Annual Festivals Calendar

Ohio is home to a vibrant and diverse array of festivals that celebrate everything from food and music to history and culture. Here's a look at some of the key annual festivals in Ohio, organized by month:

January
- Winterfest: Celebrated in various locations, this festival features ice sculptures, snow games, and winter-themed activities.

February
- Columbus Black History Month Celebration: A month-long series of events honoring African American history and culture in Columbus.

March
- Maple Syrup Festival: Held in Lucas, Richland County, this festival celebrates the maple syrup season with pancake breakfasts, syrup-making demonstrations, and more.
- Columbus Brew Festival: A popular event for craft beer enthusiasts, featuring a wide selection of brews from local and regional breweries.

April

- Ohio Pawpaw Festival: Celebrated in Albany, this festival honors the unique pawpaw fruit with tastings, cooking demonstrations, and live music.
- Springtime Tallgrass Music Festival: Held in Bellefontaine, this festival features a variety of musical performances in a beautiful outdoor setting.

May

- Buckeye Cruise-In: A classic car show held in downtown Columbus, showcasing vintage and custom cars.
- Marietta Riverfront Festival: A family-friendly event with live music, food vendors, and activities along the Ohio River.

June

- Cincinnati Music Festival: A large-scale music festival featuring a diverse lineup of artists and genres.
- Cleveland International Film Festival: A major film festival showcasing independent and international films.

July

- Cincinnati Reds Opening Day Parade: A beloved tradition celebrating the start of the baseball season with a parade and festivities.

- Ohio State Fair: Held in Columbus, this fair features rides, games, concerts, and agricultural exhibits.

August
- Ohio Brew Week: A statewide celebration of craft beer with events and tastings at breweries across the state.
- Cleveland Air Show: One of the largest air shows in the country, featuring military and civilian aircraft displays.

September
- Hocking Hills Apple Festival: Held in Logan, this festival celebrates the apple harvest with apple butter making, pie-eating contests, and more.
- Cincinnati Chili Week: A week-long celebration of Cincinnati's famous chili, with special events and tastings.

October
- Columbus Oktoberfest: A German-style festival with beer, bratwurst, and traditional Bavarian music and dance.
- Halloween Howl: A family-friendly Halloween event in Cleveland with trick-or-treating, costume contests, and spooky activities.

November
- Holiday Tree Festival: Held in Akron, this festival features beautifully decorated trees, holiday crafts, and festive activities.

- PNC Festival of Lights: A spectacular light display in Cincinnati's Fountain Square, marking the start of the holiday season.

December
- Wild Winter Lights at the Cleveland Metroparks Zoo: A dazzling light display at the zoo, perfect for a festive family outing.
- Butch Bando's Fantasy of Lights: A drive-through light show in Delaware, featuring thousands of twinkling lights and holiday displays.

Ohio's festivals offer something for everyone, from foodies and music lovers to history buffs and outdoor enthusiasts. Whether you're a local or a visitor, there's always something exciting to look forward to throughout the year.

Seasonal Events

Ohio is a state that truly embraces the changing seasons, with a variety of events and activities to celebrate the unique charm of each time of year. From winter wonderlands to summer festivals, here are some of the top seasonal events in Ohio:

Winter
- Winterfest at The Cleveland Metroparks Zoo: This magical event features light displays, ice sculptures, and holiday-themed activities.

Visitors can enjoy the zoo's animals alongside festive entertainment.
- Holiday Lights at the Toledo Zoo: A dazzling display of over one million lights transforms the zoo into a winter wonderland, complete with holiday music, Santa visits, and festive treats.
- Christmas at Clifton Mill: Known for its spectacular holiday light display, this event features millions of lights illuminating the historic mill, a miniature village, and a Santa Claus museum.

Spring
- Cherry Blossom Festival in Columbus: Held in Franklin Park Conservatory, this festival celebrates the blooming of cherry blossoms with cultural performances, food, and family-friendly activities.
- Tulip Festival at Kingwood Center Gardens: Located in Mansfield, this event showcases thousands of blooming tulips in a breathtaking display of color. Visitors can stroll through the gardens and enjoy horticultural tours.
- Cinco de Mayo Celebration in Cleveland: This lively event features traditional Mexican music, dance, and cuisine, offering a vibrant cultural experience.

Summer
- Red, White & BOOM! in Columbus: The largest Independence Day fireworks display in Ohio, this

event includes a parade, live music, and family-friendly activities along the Scioto Mile.
- Ohio State Fair in Columbus: A summer staple, the Ohio State Fair features rides, games, concerts, agricultural exhibits, and delicious fair food.
- Pro Football Hall of Fame Enshrinement Festival in Canton: This week-long celebration includes parades, concerts, and the induction ceremony for new members of the Pro Football Hall of Fame.

Fall
- Oktoberfest Zinzinnati in Cincinnati: One of the largest Oktoberfest celebrations in the United States, this event features German food, beer, music, and traditional Bavarian entertainment.
- Circleville Pumpkin Show: Known as the "Greatest Free Show on Earth," this festival celebrates all things pumpkin with parades, contests, live entertainment, and giant pumpkin displays.
- Hocking Hills Fall Festival: This festival offers a variety of autumn activities, including hayrides, pumpkin carving, and scenic hikes through the beautiful fall foliage of Hocking Hills.

What People Love About Seasonal Events in Ohio
- Festive Atmosphere: Each event brings a unique and festive atmosphere that captures the essence

of the season, making them enjoyable for all ages.
- Community Spirit: Seasonal events provide an opportunity for communities to come together, celebrate, and create lasting memories.
- Diverse Activities: From cultural festivals and parades to light displays and agricultural fairs, there is something for everyone to enjoy.
- Scenic Beauty: Many events take advantage of Ohio's natural beauty, allowing visitors to appreciate the state's landscapes and changing seasons.

Ohio's seasonal events offer a delightful way to experience the state's rich culture, traditions, and natural beauty. Whether you're celebrating the holidays, enjoying the blooms of spring, or indulging in fall festivities, there's always something exciting happening in Ohio.

Special Cultural Celebrations

Ohio is a melting pot of cultures, and its calendar is filled with vibrant festivals and events that celebrate the state's rich cultural diversity. These special cultural celebrations offer a glimpse into the traditions, food, music, and art of various communities. Here are some of the most notable cultural celebrations in Ohio:

Asian Festival (Columbus)

Key Highlights
- ☐ Cultural Performances: Enjoy traditional dance, music, and martial arts demonstrations from various Asian cultures.
- ☐ Food Vendors: A wide array of Asian cuisine, from sushi to dumplings, showcasing the flavors of different countries.
- ☐ Cultural Exhibits: Educational booths and displays that highlight the history, traditions, and contributions of Asian communities.

What People Love
- Diverse Performances: The variety of performances and activities keeps visitors entertained and engaged.

Ohio Travel Guide 2025

- Delicious Food: The opportunity to try authentic Asian dishes is a major draw for food enthusiasts.
- Educational Experience: Visitors appreciate the chance to learn about different cultures and traditions.

Oktoberfest Zinzinnati (Cincinnati)

Key Highlights
- Authentic German Food and Beer: Traditional German dishes like bratwurst, schnitzel, and pretzels, along with a wide selection of beers.
- Bavarian Entertainment: Live music, folk dances, and the famous chicken dance add to the festive atmosphere.
- Parade and Contests: Events like the Running of the Wieners (dachshund race) and stein-holding competitions provide fun for all ages.

What People Love
- Festive Atmosphere: The lively, fun-filled environment is perfect for celebrating with friends and family.
- Cultural Immersion: Attendees enjoy the authentic German experiences, from food to music.
- Community Spirit: The event brings people together, fostering a sense of community and shared joy.

Greek Festival (Cleveland)

Key Highlights
- Traditional Greek Food: Savory dishes like gyros, moussaka, and baklava, prepared by local Greek families.

- Cultural Performances: Greek music, dance performances, and traditional folk attire.
- Marketplaces: Vendors offering Greek crafts, jewelry, and other handmade items.

What People Love
- Authentic Cuisine: Visitors rave about the delicious, homemade Greek food.
- Welcoming Community: The friendly and inviting atmosphere makes everyone feel part of the celebration.
- Cultural Insight: The festival provides a rich cultural experience, highlighting the traditions and heritage of the Greek community.

Hispanic Heritage Month Festival (Dayton)

Key Highlights
- Live Music and Dance: Performances by mariachi bands, salsa dancers, and other Hispanic artists.
- Food Trucks and Stalls: A variety of Hispanic cuisines, from tacos and empanadas to churros and flan.
- Cultural Exhibits: Displays and activities that celebrate the contributions and history of Hispanic communities.

What People Love
- Vibrant Performances: The lively music and dance performances are a highlight for many attendees.
- Tasty Food: The diverse selection of Hispanic foods is a big attraction for food lovers.
- Inclusive Atmosphere: The festival's welcoming and inclusive spirit makes it a great event for everyone.

Italian Festival (Columbus)

Key Highlights
- Italian Cuisine: Enjoy classic Italian dishes like pasta, pizza, and cannoli, prepared by local chefs.
- Entertainment: Live Italian music, bocce ball tournaments, and traditional folk dances.
- Parade and Processions: Colorful parades featuring floats, marching bands, and cultural displays.

What People Love
- Delicious Food: The authentic Italian cuisine is a major draw for visitors.
- Family-Friendly Activities: The festival offers a variety of activities and games for all ages.
- Rich Cultural Experience: Attendees appreciate the celebration of Italian culture and heritage.

Ohio's special cultural celebrations offer a wonderful opportunity to experience the state's diverse communities and traditions. Whether you're tasting new foods, enjoying live performances, or learning about different cultures, these festivals provide a rich and enjoyable experience for all.

CHAPTER 12: SAMPLE ITINERARIES

Weekend Getaway in Columbus

Whether you're a first-time visitor or a returning traveler, Columbus offers a vibrant mix of activities, dining, and attractions that make for an unforgettable weekend getaway. Here's a detailed itinerary to help you make the most of your weekend in Ohio's capital city:

Friday

Evening: Arrival and Check-In
- Hotel Options: Consider staying at The Joseph, a Le Méridien Hotel for a luxurious experience, or Drury Inn & Suites Columbus Convention Center for a comfortable and centrally located option.
- Dinner: Head to The Pearl in the Short North Arts District for a delicious dinner. This modern American restaurant is known for its oysters, craft beers, and hearty comfort food.

Night: Explore the Short North
- Short North Arts District: Stroll through this vibrant neighborhood, known for its galleries, boutiques, and nightlife. Check out local art, browse unique shops, and maybe grab a drink at one of the many bars.

Saturday

Morning: Breakfast and Outdoor Activities
- Breakfast: Start your day with a hearty breakfast at Fox in the Snow Cafe. Known for its pastries and coffee, this cafe is a local favorite.
- Outdoor Adventure: Spend the morning exploring the Scioto Mile, a collection of parks and trails along the downtown riverfront. Enjoy a walk or bike ride with scenic views of the city and the river.

Mid-Morning: Visit COSI
- COSI (Center of Science and Industry): Spend a few hours at this interactive science museum. It's perfect for visitors of all ages with exhibits ranging from space exploration to ocean life.

Lunch: North Market
- North Market: Head to this historic public market for a diverse selection of food vendors offering everything from international cuisine to local specialties. Enjoy lunch and maybe pick up some souvenirs.

Afternoon: Cultural Exploration
- Columbus Museum of Art: Spend the afternoon exploring the Columbus Museum of Art. The museum features a diverse collection of American and European art, as well as rotating special exhibits.

- Franklin Park Conservatory and Botanical Gardens: If you have time, visit this beautiful conservatory filled with exotic plants, seasonal displays, and a stunning butterfly exhibit.

Evening: Dinner and Entertainment
- Dinner: Enjoy a sumptuous dinner at Lindey's, an upscale bistro in the German Village known for its classic American dishes and elegant atmosphere.
- Nightlife: Catch a show at the Columbus Symphony Orchestra or enjoy live music at Natalie's Coal Fired Pizza and Live Music. If you prefer comedy, check out a performance at the Funny Bone Comedy Club.

Sunday

Morning: Breakfast and Local Exploration
- Breakfast: Start your day with breakfast at Skillet, a farm-to-table restaurant known for its seasonal dishes and hearty breakfasts.
- Explore German Village: Spend the morning wandering around German Village, a historic neighborhood with charming brick streets, unique shops, and beautiful homes. Don't miss The Book Loft, a 32-room bookstore that's a book lover's paradise.

Mid-Morning: Columbus Zoo and Aquarium
- Columbus Zoo and Aquarium: Visit one of the top-rated zoos in the country. The zoo features a wide variety of animals and exhibits, perfect for a fun and educational experience.

Lunch: Easton Town Center
- Easton Town Center: Head to this popular shopping and entertainment complex for lunch. Choose from a variety of dining options, including Northstar Cafe for healthy, organic fare or Brio Tuscan Grille for Italian cuisine.

Afternoon: Shopping and Departure
- Shopping: Spend some time exploring the shops at Easton Town Center or head back to the Short North for more boutique shopping.
- Departure: After a weekend of exploration and fun, check out of your hotel and head home with wonderful memories of your time in Columbus.

This itinerary provides a blend of culture, outdoor activities, dining, and entertainment, ensuring a well-rounded and enjoyable weekend in Columbus. Whether you're traveling solo, as a couple, or with family, there's something for everyone to enjoy.

One-Week Road Trip Through Ohio

Ohio is a state rich in history, natural beauty, and vibrant cities. A road trip through Ohio offers a wonderful mix of urban adventures, scenic landscapes, and cultural experiences. Here's a detailed one-week itinerary for an unforgettable road trip through Ohio:

Day 1: Cincinnati

Morning: Arrival and Explore Downtown
- Breakfast: Start your trip with breakfast at Taste of Belgium, known for its delicious waffles.
- Fountain Square: Visit this central gathering spot, featuring the iconic Tyler Davidson Fountain.

Mid-Morning: Visit Over-the-Rhine
- Findlay Market: Explore Ohio's oldest continuously operated public market, offering a variety of fresh produce and local foods.
- Washington Park: Enjoy a leisurely stroll in this beautifully landscaped park.

Afternoon: Cultural Exploration
- Cincinnati Art Museum: Discover a diverse collection of art spanning 6,000 years.
- Lunch: Grab a bite at Maplewood Kitchen and Bar, offering a fresh and healthy menu.

Evening: Dinner and Music
- Dinner: Head to Jeff Ruby's Steakhouse for a top-notch dining experience.
- Music Hall: Enjoy a performance by the Cincinnati Symphony Orchestra if available.

Day 2: Cincinnati to Dayton

Morning: National Museum of the US Air Force
- Drive to Dayton: About a 1-hour drive north.
- National Museum of the US Air Force: Spend the morning exploring the world's largest military aviation museum.

Afternoon: Carillon Historical Park
- Lunch: Enjoy lunch at the Carillon Brewing Company within the park.
- Explore Carillon Historical Park: Learn about Dayton's industrial and aviation history.

Evening Relax and Dine
- Check-In: Stay at The Inn at the Park in Dayton.
- Dinner: Dine at Salar Restaurant and Lounge, offering a fusion of world cuisines.

Day 3: Dayton to Columbus

Morning: Ohio History Center and Ohio Village
- Drive to Columbus: Approximately 1-hour drive east.
- Ohio History Center: Explore exhibits on Ohio's history and culture.
- Ohio Village: A recreated 19th-century village adjacent to the mu:seum.

Afternoon: Lunch and Science
- Lunch: Eat at Northstar Cafe in the Short North area.
- COSI (Center of Science and Industry): Spend the afternoon at this interactive science museum.

Evening: German Village
- Check-In: Stay at The German Village Guest House.
- Dinner: Dine at Lindey's for an upscale dining experience in German Village.
- Book Loft: End the evening browsing the 32-room bookstore in German Village.

Day 4: Columbus to Hocking Hills

Morning: Franklin Park Conservatory and Botanical Gardens
- Franklin Park Conservatory: Explore the beautiful botanical gardens and exhibits.

Mid-Morning: Drive to Hocking Hills
- Drive to Hocking Hills: About a 1.5-hour drive southeast.

Afternoon: Nature and Adventure
- Check-In: Stay at Inn & Spa at Cedar Falls.
- Hiking: Explore the trails of Old Man's Cave, one of Hocking Hills' most popular attractions.

Evening: Relax and Unwind
- Dinner: Enjoy dinner at the Inn & Spa at Cedar Falls restaurant, known for its farm-to-table cuisine.
- Stargazing: Take advantage of the dark skies in Hocking Hills for some stargazing.

Day 5: Hocking Hills to Amish Country

Morning: Hocking Hills Canopy Tours
- Zip-lining: Start your day with an adrenaline rush on a zip-lining tour through the forest.

Mid-Morning: Drive to Amish Country
- Drive to Amish Country: About a 2-hour drive northeast.

Afternoon: Explore Berlin and Millersburg
- Check-In: Stay at The Inn at Honey Run in Millersburg.
- Amish Culture: Visit local shops and bakeries in Berlin and Millersburg.
- Yoder's Amish Home: Take a tour of an Amish home and learn about their way of life.

Evening: Dinner and Relaxation
- Dinner: Enjoy a hearty meal at Der Dutchman in Walnut Creek, known for its Amish-style cooking.

Day 6: Amish Country to Cleveland

Morning: Explore Local Markets
- Amish Markets: Visit farmers' markets and pick up some local Amish produce and crafts.

Mid-Morning: Drive to Cleveland
- Drive to Cleveland: About a 1.5-hour drive north.

Afternoon: Cultural Sites
- Rock & Roll Hall of Fame: Spend the afternoon exploring exhibits on the history of rock and roll.
- Lunch: Grab a bite at the Great Lakes Brewing Company.

Evening: Dinner and Entertainment
- Check-In: Stay at Hilton Cleveland Downtown.
- Dinner: Dine at Lola Bistro, one of Cleveland's top restaurants.
- Playhouse Square: Catch a show at one of the theaters in the second-largest performing arts center in the U.S.

Day 7: Cleveland to Toledo

Morning: Cleveland Museum of Art
- Cleveland Museum of Art: Explore one of the finest art collections in the country.

Mid-Morning: Drive to Toledo
- Drive to Toledo: About a 2-hour drive west.

Afternoon: Toledo Zoo and Aquarium
- Toledo Zoo and Aquarium: Spend the afternoon visiting the zoo and aquarium, known for its diverse exhibits.

Evening: Dinner and Farewell
- Check-In: Stay at Renaissance Toledo Downtown Hotel.
- Dinner: Enjoy dinner at The Real Seafood Company, offering fresh seafood and great views of the Maumee River.

This one-week road trip through Ohio offers a mix of urban excitement, cultural experiences, and natural beauty, ensuring a memorable journey.

Family Vacation Itinerary

Ohio is a fantastic destination for a family vacation, offering a variety of activities and attractions that cater to all ages. From exciting amusement parks to educational museums and beautiful natural parks, there's something for everyone to enjoy. Here's a detailed one-week itinerary for a memorable family vacation in Ohio:

Day 1: Cleveland

Morning: Arrival and Check-In
- Hotel Options: Stay at Drury Plaza Hotel Cleveland Downtown for a family-friendly atmosphere and convenient location.

Mid-Morning: Cleveland Metroparks Zoo
- Cleveland Metroparks Zoo: Start your adventure with a visit to the zoo, home to a wide variety of animals and interactive exhibits.

Afternoon: Great Lakes Science Center
- Lunch: Grab a quick bite at the zoo before heading to your next destination.
- Great Lakes Science Center: Explore hands-on science exhibits and the NASA Glenn Visitor Center, perfect for curious minds.

Evening: Dinner and Relaxation
- Dinner: Dine at Melt Bar and Grilled, known for its creative grilled cheese sandwiches that kids will love.
- Relax: Spend the evening relaxing at the hotel pool or enjoying family-friendly activities nearby.

Day 2: Cleveland to Sandusky

Morning: Rock & Roll Hall of Fame
- Rock & Roll Hall of Fame: Visit this iconic museum and enjoy exhibits that showcase the history of rock and roll.

Mid-Morning: Drive to Sandusky
- Drive to Sandusky: About a 1-hour drive west.

Afternoon: Cedar Point Amusement Park
- Lunch: Eat at one of the many dining options within the park.
- Cedar Point: Spend the afternoon enjoying the thrilling rides, family-friendly attractions, and live entertainment at one of the world's best amusement parks.

Evening: Check-In and Dinner
- Hotel Options: Stay at Cedar Point's Hotel Breakers for convenient access to the park.
- Dinner: Enjoy dinner at one of the park's restaurants or nearby eateries.

Day 3: Sandusky to Columbus

Morning: Kalahari Resorts
- Kalahari Resorts: Start your day with some water park fun at Kalahari Resorts, which offers both indoor and outdoor water attractions.

Mid-Morning: Drive to Columbus
- Drive to Columbus: About a 2-hour drive southeast.

Afternoon: COSI (Center of Science and Industry)
- Lunch: Have lunch at North Market in Columbus.
- COSI: Spend the afternoon at this interactive science museum, with exhibits ranging from space exploration to hands-on experiments for kids.

Evening: Dinner and German Village
- Hotel Options: Stay at Hilton Columbus Downtown for a family-friendly experience.
- Dinner: Head to Schmidt's Sausage Haus in German Village for a delicious meal in a historic setting.
- Explore German Village: Wander the charming streets and visit The Book Loft, a 32-room bookstore that's perfect for browsing.

Day 4: Columbus

Morning: Columbus Zoo and Aquarium
- Columbus Zoo and Aquarium: Spend the morning exploring one of the top-rated zoos in the country, with a wide variety of animals and exhibits.

Afternoon: Franklin Park Conservatory
- Lunch: Enjoy lunch at the zoo before heading to your next destination.
- Franklin Park Conservatory and Botanical Gardens: Explore the beautiful gardens, plant collections, and seasonal displays.

Evening: Dinner and Movie Night
- Dinner: Dine at Mellow Mushroom for a family-friendly atmosphere and great pizza.
- Movie Night: Catch a family movie at Gateway Film Center or relax at the hotel.

Day 5: Columbus to Hocking Hills

Morning: Drive to Hocking Hills
- Drive to Hocking Hills: About a 1.5-hour drive southeast.

Afternoon: Outdoor Adventures
- Check-In: Stay at Inn & Spa at Cedar Falls or rent a family cabin.
- Old Man's Cave: Enjoy a family hike through the stunning landscapes of Old Man's Cave.

Evening: Dinner and Campfire
- Dinner: Have dinner at the Inn & Spa at Cedar Falls restaurant.
- Campfire: Spend the evening around a campfire, roasting marshmallows and sharing stories.

Day 6: Hocking Hills to Cincinnati

Morning: Outdoor Activities
- Zip-lining: Try zip-lining at Hocking Hills Canopy Tours for an adventurous start to your day.

Mid-Morning: Drive to Cincinnati
- Drive to Cincinnati: About a 2-hour drive southwest.

Afternoon: Newport Aquarium
- Check-In: Stay at The Westin Cincinnati for a convenient and comfortable stay.
- Newport Aquarium: Visit the aquarium and marvel at the underwater exhibits and interactive displays.

Evening: Dinner and Fountain Square
- Dinner: Dine at Taste of Belgium for a family-friendly dining experience.
- Fountain Square: Enjoy the lively atmosphere, live music, and interactive fountains.

Day 7: Cincinnati

Morning: Cincinnati Children's Museum
- Cincinnati Children's Museum: Spend the morning exploring interactive exhibits and educational displays perfect for kids.

Afternoon: Kings Island
- Lunch: Grab lunch at the museum or nearby restaurant.
- Kings Island: Spend the afternoon at this popular amusement park, enjoying rides and attractions for all ages.

Evening: Farewell Dinner
- Dinner: Enjoy a farewell dinner at Montgomery Inn Boathouse, known for its delicious ribs and riverfront views.

This family vacation itinerary offers a mix of educational, adventurous, and fun activities that will create lasting memories for everyone.

Adventure Seeker's Guide

Ohio is a playground for adventure seekers, offering a wide range of thrilling activities. This one-week itinerary is designed to give you a taste of the best adventure experiences the Buckeye State has to offer:

Day 1: Cleveland

Morning: Arrival and Check-In
- Hotel Options: Stay at Drury Plaza Hotel Cleveland Downtown for a central location and great amenities.

Mid-Morning: Cleveland Metroparks Zoo
- Cleveland Metroparks Zoo: Start your adventure with a visit to the zoo, home to a diverse range of animals and interactive exhibits.

Afternoon: Rock & Roll Hall of Fame
- Rock & Roll Hall of Fame: Explore exhibits on the history of rock and roll, and enjoy the vibrant atmosphere.

Evening: Dinner and Relaxation
- Dinner: Dine at Mabel's BBQ for some delicious, smoky barbecue.
- Relax: Unwind at your hotel or explore downtown Cleveland's nightlife.

Day 2: Cleveland to Hocking Hills

Morning: Drive to Hocking Hills
- Drive to Hocking Hills: Approximately a 3-hour drive south.

Afternoon: Hocking Hills Canopy Tours
- Zip-Lining: Experience the thrill of flying through the treetops with Hocking Hills Canopy Tours.

Evening: Check-In and Dinner
- Check-In: Stay at Inn & Spa at Cedar Falls or a nearby cabin.

- Dinner: Enjoy a cozy dinner at the Inn & Spa at Cedar Falls restaurant.

Day 3: Hocking Hills

Morning: Hiking Adventures
- Old Man's Cave: Hike through the beautiful Old Man's Cave trails, known for its stunning rock formations and waterfalls.

Afternoon: Rock Climbing
- Rock Climbing: Test your skills at the High Rock Adventures climbing park, offering various climbing routes for different skill levels.

Evening: Campfire and Stargazing
- Campfire: Enjoy a campfire dinner and roast marshmallows.
- Stargazing: Take advantage of the dark skies in Hocking Hills for some incredible stargazing.

Day 4: Hocking Hills to Dayton

Morning: Drive to Dayton
- Drive to Dayton: Approximately a 2-hour drive west.

Afternoon: National Museum of the US Air Force
- Museum Visit: Explore the world's largest military aviation museum, with exhibits ranging from early flight to space exploration.

Evening: Carillon Historical Park
- Carillon Historical Park: Discover Dayton's industrial and aviation history.
- Dinner: Dine at Carillon Brewing Company within the park.

Day 5: Dayton to Mohican State Park

Morning: Drive to Mohican State Park
- Drive to Mohican State Park: Approximately a 2-hour drive northeast.

Afternoon: Mountain Biking
- Mountain Biking: Tackle the trails of the Mohican Mountain Bike Trail, offering a mix of challenging terrain and scenic beauty.

Evening: Check-In and Relax
- Check-In: Stay at Mohican Lodge & Conference Center.
- Dinner: Enjoy dinner at the lodge restaurant and unwind by the fire.

Day 6: Mohican State Park to Columbus

Morning: Canoeing on the Mohican River
- Canoeing: Spend the morning canoeing on the Mohican River, enjoying the tranquil waters and lush surroundings.

Mid-Morning: Drive to Columbus
- Drive to Columbus: Approximately a 1.5-hour drive southwest.

Afternoon: Skydiving
- Skydiving: Experience the ultimate thrill with a tandem skydive at Skydive Columbus.

Evening: Dinner and German Village
- Hotel Options: Stay at Hilton Columbus Downtown.
- Dinner: Dine at Lindey's in German Village for an upscale dining experience.
- Explore German Village: Wander the charming streets and visit The Book Loft.

Day 7: Columbus to Cincinnati

Morning: White-Water Rafting
- Drive to Cincinnati: Approximately a 2-hour drive southwest.
- White-Water Rafting on the Great Miami River: Take on the rapids of the Great Miami River for an adrenaline-pumping adventure.

Afternoon: Newport Aquarium
- Newport Aquarium: Explore the underwater exhibits and interactive displays at the aquarium.

Evening: Farewell Dinner
- Hotel Options: Stay at The Westin Cincinnati.
- Dinner: Enjoy a farewell dinner at Montgomery Inn Boathouse, known for its delicious ribs and riverfront views.

This adventure-packed itinerary promises an unforgettable week of thrills and excitement across Ohio. From zip-lining and rock climbing to skydiving and white-water rafting, there's something for every adventure seeker.

CHAPTER 13: DAY TRIPS AND NEARBY ATTRACTIONS

Ohio's Amish Country

Ohio's Amish Country offers a peaceful escape with its picturesque landscapes, charming villages, and traditional Amish lifestyle. Here's a guide to experiencing the best of Ohio's Amish Country:

Key Highlights

Scenic Beauty
- Rolling Hills and Farmlands: Enjoy lush, rolling hills and expansive farmlands.
- Covered Bridges: Explore charming covered bridges for great photo ops.

Amish Culture and Traditions

- Horse-Drawn Buggies: Experience the iconic Amish transportation.
- Amish Crafts and Quilts: Find beautiful handmade quilts and crafts in local shops.

Delicious Amish Cuisine

- Hearty Home-Cooked Meals: Enjoy traditional dishes like roast chicken and homemade bread.
- Bakery Goods: Savor freshly baked pies and cookies from local bakeries.

What People Love About Amish Country

Authentic Experiences

- Farm Visits: Tour Amish farms and learn about their way of life.
- Buggy Rides: Take a relaxing buggy ride through the countryside.

Peaceful Atmosphere

- Quiet Retreat: Enjoy the serene environment and slower pace of life.
- Friendly Locals: Experience the warmth and hospitality of the Amish community.

Must-Visit Locations in Amish Country

Berlin
- Antique Mall: Find unique souvenirs at the Berlin Village Antique Mall.
- Farmstead Restaurant: Enjoy delicious Amish cuisine.

Millersburg
- Yoder's Amish Home: Tour an authentic Amish home and learn about their culture.
- Millersburg Brewing Company: Taste local craft beer.

Walnut Creek
- Coblentz Chocolate Company: Indulge in hand-crafted chocolates.
- Walnut Creek Cheese: Shop for Amish-made cheeses and baked goods.

Seasonal Events and Festivals

Fall Harvest Festivals
- Holmes County Amish Country Fall Festival: Celebrate the harvest with live music and crafts.
- Amish Country Theater: Enjoy live performances and comedy shows.

Christmas in Amish Country
- Holiday Shopping: Find unique gifts and decorations.

- Light Displays: Experience festive light displays in the countryside.

Ohio's Amish Country offers a blend of culture, scenic beauty, and warm hospitality. Whether you're interested in Amish traditions, enjoying homemade food, or soaking in the peaceful surroundings, Amish Country provides a memorable experience.

Geneva-on-the-Lake

Geneva-on-the-Lake, located on the shores of Lake Erie, is Ohio's original summer resort. This charming village offers a nostalgic getaway with a mix of outdoor activities, scenic views, and vintage charm. Here's a guide to experiencing the best of Geneva-on-the-Lake:

Key Highlights

Scenic Beauty
- Lake Erie Shoreline: Enjoy stunning views of Lake Erie, especially during sunrise and sunset.
- Geneva State Park: Explore the park's trails, marina, and beach for a variety of outdoor activities.

Vintage Charm
- Strip: The heart of Geneva-on-the-Lake is its vintage strip, lined with arcades, mini-golf courses, diners, and shops, providing a nostalgic feel.

Local Wineries
- Wine Tasting: The region is known for its wineries. Visit local favorites like Old Firehouse Winery and The Lakehouse Inn & Winery for tastings and tours.

What People Love About Geneva-on-the-Lake

Family-Friendly Activities
- Adventure Zone: A fun-filled amusement park with go-karts, bumper boats, mini-golf, and a climbing wall.
- Lake Erie Canopy Tours: Experience the thrill of zip-lining with views of the lake and forest.

Relaxing Atmosphere
- Beaches and Parks: Spend the day lounging on the beach or picnicking in Geneva State Park.
- Lakeside Dining: Enjoy fresh seafood and lake views at eateries like Eddie's Grill and The Lakehouse Inn Restaurant.

Must-Visit Locations

Geneva State Park
- Marina: Rent a boat or take a scenic cruise on Lake Erie.
- Trails: Hike or bike the trails that wind through the park, offering beautiful views of the lake and wildlife.

The Strip
- Eddie's Grill: A classic 1950s-style diner known for its hot dogs, root beer floats, and retro atmosphere.
- Firehouse Winery: Enjoy wine with a view at this lakeside winery, complete with a Ferris wheel.

Seasonal Events and Festivals

Summer Concerts and Festivals
- Thunder on the Strip: A popular motorcycle rally held in September, featuring live music and events.

- Summer Concert Series: Enjoy live music at Geneva State Park and other local venues throughout the summer.

Fall Events
- Wine Tasting Tours: Take advantage of the fall harvest season to explore local wineries and sample the latest vintages.
- Autumn Leaves Festival: Celebrate the changing seasons with craft vendors, food, and entertainment.

Geneva-on-the-Lake offers a perfect blend of relaxation, adventure, and nostalgia. Whether you're enjoying water activities, exploring the vintage strip, or sipping wine at a local winery, this lakeside resort provides a charming and memorable experience.

Ohio State Reformatory in Mansfield

The Ohio State Reformatory, located in Mansfield, Ohio, is one of the state's most iconic and historic landmarks. Known for its stunning architecture and storied past, this former prison offers a unique and intriguing experience for visitors. Here's a guide to exploring the Ohio State Reformatory:

Key Highlights

Historic Architecture
- Gothic Revival Design: The reformatory's architecture is a blend of Victorian Gothic, Richardsonian Romanesque, and Queen Anne styles, creating a striking and imposing structure.
- Grand Entrance Hall: The entrance hall features intricate woodwork, a grand staircase, and beautiful stained glass windows.

Film Location
- The Shawshank Redemption: The Ohio State Reformatory is famously known as the primary filming location for the 1994 film "The Shawshank Redemption." Fans of the movie can tour key filming sites within the prison.

What People Love About the Ohio State Reformatory

Guided Tours
- History Meets Hollywood Tour: This tour highlights the prison's history as well as its role in "The Shawshank Redemption."
- Ghost Hunts: For those interested in the paranormal, the reformatory offers guided ghost hunts and overnight stays, as it is rumored to be haunted.

Historical Exhibits
- Prison Cells: Visitors can explore the reformatory's cellblocks, including the East Cell Block, which is the largest free-standing steel cell block in the world.
- Museum Rooms: The reformatory features exhibits on its history, notable inmates, and the prison's role in pop culture.

Must-Visit Locations

The Chapel
- Beautifully Preserved: The chapel remains one of the most well-preserved parts of the reformatory and often serves as a venue for events.

Warden's Office
- Authentic Furnishings: The office is furnished to reflect its appearance during the prison's operation and includes displays on the wardens who served there.

Solitary Confinement
- Haunting Experience: A visit to the solitary confinement area offers a glimpse into the harsh conditions faced by inmates.

Seasonal Events and Festivals

Incarceration Festival
- Rock and Metal Music: This summer music festival features rock and metal bands and attracts fans from across the country.
- Tours and Activities: Festival attendees can also take guided tours of the reformatory and participate in various activities.

Halloween Events
- Blood Prison: During the Halloween season, the reformatory transforms into a haunted house attraction, offering a thrilling and spooky experience.

The Ohio State Reformatory offers a fascinating look into history, architecture, and pop culture, making it a must-visit destination for anyone interested in these areas. Whether you're exploring its historic halls, reliving scenes from "The Shawshank Redemption," or searching for ghosts, the reformatory provides a unique and memorable experience.

Serpent Mound Historical Site

The Serpent Mound, located in Adams County, Ohio, is one of the most intriguing prehistoric effigy mounds in North America. This remarkable earthwork, built by ancient indigenous peoples, offers a unique glimpse into the region's ancient history and culture. Here's a guide to exploring the Serpent Mound Historical Site:

Key Highlights

The Effigy Mound
- Serpent Shape: The mound is shaped like an uncoiling serpent, stretching over 1,300 feet in length and averaging three feet in height. The serpent's head is aligned with the summer solstice sunset, adding to its enigmatic nature.

- Ancient Origins: Though its exact origins are debated, it is generally attributed to the Adena culture (800 BCE to 100 CE) or the Fort Ancient culture (1000 CE to 1650 CE).

Interpretive Center
- Educational Exhibits: The on-site museum features exhibits on the history, culture, and significance of the mound, including artifacts from the prehistoric peoples who built it.
- Interactive Displays: Visitors can explore interactive displays that explain the construction and purpose of effigy mounds.

What People Love About the Serpent Mound

Historical Significance
- Ancient Mysteries: The Serpent Mound is a site of great archaeological and historical importance, providing insights into the ceremonial practices of ancient indigenous cultures.
- Solar Alignments: The mound's alignment with celestial events like the summer solstice sunset fascinates visitors and adds to its mystique.

Scenic Beauty
- Natural Surroundings: The site is located in a picturesque park with rolling hills and lush greenery, offering a serene environment for exploration.

- Walking Trails: Trails around the mound allow visitors to view the effigy from different angles and appreciate its scale and craftsmanship.

Must-Visit Locations at Serpent Mound

The Observation Tower
- Panoramic Views: Climb the observation tower for a bird's-eye view of the entire serpent-shaped mound and its surroundings.

The Head of the Serpent
- Celestial Alignment: Stand at the head of the serpent to appreciate its alignment with the sunset during the summer solstice.

The Interpretive Center
- Educational Experience: Spend time in the interpretive center to learn about the construction, cultural significance, and various theories surrounding the mound.

Seasonal Events and Activities

Summer Solstice Celebration
- Astronomical Alignment: Join fellow visitors during the summer solstice to witness the mound's alignment with the sunset. This event often includes guided tours and educational talks.

Fall Foliage Tours
- Scenic Beauty: Visit during the fall to enjoy the beautiful autumn colors that enhance the natural beauty of the site.

Educational Programs
- Workshops and Lectures: Throughout the year, the Serpent Mound Historical Site offers workshops, lectures, and educational programs focused on archaeology, astronomy, and indigenous cultures.

The Serpent Mound Historical Site is a destination that combines natural beauty with historical intrigue. Whether you're fascinated by ancient history, interested in archaeology, or simply looking to explore a unique cultural landmark, the Serpent Mound offers a captivating experience.

CHAPTER 14: TRAVEL RESOURCES

Comprehensive List of Emergency Contacts

It's crucial to have a list of emergency contacts readily available to ensure safety and quick response in case of emergencies. Here's a comprehensive list of emergency contacts that will be helpful and useful for various situations:

Emergency Services
- Emergency (Police, Fire, Ambulance): 911

Medical Assistance
- Poison Control Center: 1-800-222-1222
- National Suicide Prevention Lifeline: 988
- American Red Cross: 1-800-733-2767
- Local Hospital: Add the contact details of the nearest hospital to your location.

Local Utilities and Services
- Gas Company Emergency: Add the contact details of your local gas company emergency line.
- Electric Company Emergency: Add the contact details of your local electric company emergency line.
- Water Company Emergency: Add the contact details of your local water company emergency line.

Travel and Roadside Assistance
- AAA Roadside Assistance: 1-800-222-4357
- Local Towing Service: Add the contact details of a reliable local towing service.
- Highway Patrol: Add the contact details of your state or local highway patrol.

Government and Community Services
- Non-Emergency Police Line: Add the contact details of your local non-emergency police line.
- Local Fire Department (Non-Emergency): Add the contact details of your local fire department non-emergency line.
- City or County Services: Add the contact details for your local city or county services department.

Health and Mental Health Services
- Local Health Department: Add the contact details of your local health department.
- Mental Health Crisis Line: Add the contact details of your local mental health crisis line.
- Domestic Violence Hotline: 1-800-799-7233 (SAFE)

Pet Emergencies
- Local Veterinary Clinic: Add the contact details of your local veterinary clinic.
- Pet Poison Helpline: 1-855-764-7661

Personal Contacts
- Family Members: Add contact details for immediate family members.
- Close Friends: Add contact details for close friends or neighbors who can assist in emergencies.
- Workplace Contacts: Add contact details for your workplace's emergency contact person.

Insurance Contacts
- Health Insurance: Add the contact details of your health insurance provider.
- Auto Insurance: Add the contact details of your auto insurance provider.
- Homeowners/Renters Insurance: Add the contact details of your homeowners or renters insurance provider.

Important Notes
- Local Contacts: Customize this list with contacts specific to your location.
- Regular Updates: Regularly update your list to ensure all contact information is current and accurate.
- Accessibility: Keep this list accessible in multiple places, such as your phone, wallet, and home.

Having these emergency contacts readily available can provide peace of mind and ensure you're prepared to handle various emergency situations effectively.

Traveler Resources and Websites

Planning a trip can be exciting but also requires careful consideration and preparation. To make your travel experience smoother and more enjoyable, here's a list of valuable traveler resources and websites that can help with various aspects of your journey:

General Travel Planning

TripAdvisor
- Website: www.tripadvisor.com
- What It Offers: Reviews, ratings, and travel advice on hotels, restaurants, attractions, and activities from travelers around the world.

Expedia
- Website: www.expedia.com
- What It Offers: Booking for flights, hotels, car rentals, and vacation packages, with competitive prices and special deals.

Flight Booking and Information

Skyscanner
- Website: www.skyscanner.com
- What It Offers: A powerful search engine for comparing flights from various airlines, finding the best deals, and booking tickets.

FlightAware
- Website: www.flightaware.com
- What It Offers: Real-time flight tracking, flight status updates, and airport delays information.

Accommodation

Booking.com
- Website: www.booking.com
- What It Offers: A wide range of accommodation options, including hotels, hostels, vacation rentals, and more, with user reviews and flexible booking options.

Airbnb
- Website: www.airbnb.com
- What It Offers: Unique lodging options, including private homes, apartments, and specialty stays like treehouses and yurts.

Local Transportation

Rome2rio
- Website: www.rome2rio.com
- What It Offers: Comprehensive information on how to get from one place to another using different modes of transport, including planes, trains, buses, ferries, and driving routes.

Uber/Lyft
- Websites: www.uber.com and www.lyft.com

- **What They Offer:** Ride-sharing services available in many cities around the world, providing a convenient and flexible transportation option.

Travel Insurance

World Nomads
- Website: www.worldnomads.com
- What It Offers: Travel insurance plans tailored for different types of travelers, including coverage for medical emergencies, trip cancellations, and lost belongings.

Allianz Travel Insurance
- Website: www.allianztravelinsurance.com
- What It Offers: Comprehensive travel insurance options with various coverage levels to suit different travel needs.

Health and Safety

CDC Travelers' Health
- Website: www.cdc.gov/travel
- What It Offers: Up-to-date information on travel health, including vaccinations, disease outbreaks, and travel advisories.

U.S. Department of State – Travel Advisories
- Website: travel.state.gov

- What It Offers: Travel advisories, country information, and emergency assistance for U.S. travelers abroad.

Language and Communication

Duolingo
- Website: www.duolingo.com
- What It Offers: Free language learning app and website to help you learn and practice new languages before and during your trip.

Google Translate
- Website: translate.google.com
- What It Offers: Instant translation of text, speech, and images in multiple languages, useful for overcoming language barriers while traveling.

Local Activities and Tours

Viator
- Website: www.viator.com
- What It Offers: Booking platform for local tours, activities, and experiences in various destinations worldwide.

GetYourGuide
- Website: www.getyourguide.com
- What It Offers: A wide selection of tours, activities, and tickets for attractions, with user reviews and easy booking options.

Using these traveler resources and websites can help you plan a smooth, safe, and enjoyable trip. From booking flights and accommodations to finding local activities and ensuring your health and safety, these tools cover all aspects of travel planning.

Budgeting and Cost Estimation

Effective budgeting and cost estimation are key to ensuring a smooth and enjoyable travel experience. By planning your finances carefully, you can avoid unexpected expenses and make the most of your trip. Here's a comprehensive guide to budgeting and cost estimation for travel:

Pre-Trip Budget Planning

Determine Your Travel Goals
- Destination: Decide where you want to go and the main attractions you want to see.
- Duration: Determine how long your trip will be, including travel days.

Research Costs
- Transportation: Look up the costs of flights, trains, buses, or car rentals.
- Accommodation: Check prices for hotels, hostels, vacation rentals, or other lodging options.
- Daily Expenses: Estimate costs for meals, local transportation, entrance fees, and activities.

Budget Categories

Transportation
- Flights: Compare prices on websites like Skyscanner and Expedia.
- Local Transportation: Include costs for taxis, ride-sharing, public transit, and rental cars.
- Fuel and Parking: If driving, estimate fuel costs and parking fees.

Accommodation
- Hotels and Hostels: Use booking sites like Booking.com or Airbnb to find the best deals.
- Additional Fees: Consider taxes, resort fees, or cleaning fees.

Food and Drinks
- Daily Meals: Budget for breakfast, lunch, and dinner, considering the average cost of eating out in your destination.
- Groceries: If you plan to cook, estimate the cost of groceries.
- Snacks and Drinks: Include costs for coffee, snacks, and drinks.

Activities and Entertainment
- Attraction Tickets: Look up the prices for museums, tours, and other attractions.
- Events: Include costs for any special events or shows you want to attend.

- Recreational Activities: Consider costs for activities like skiing, diving, or hiking permits.

Miscellaneous
- Travel Insurance: Budget for travel insurance to cover medical emergencies, trip cancellations, and lost belongings.
- Souvenirs and Shopping: Allocate funds for souvenirs and shopping.
- Tips and Gratuities: Include tips for service providers such as waitstaff, hotel staff, and guides.

Budgeting Tools

Travel Budget Apps
- TripIt: An app that helps you organize your travel plans and expenses.
- Trail Wallet: A budget tracking app designed specifically for travelers.

Spreadsheets
- Budget Template: Create a detailed budget using spreadsheet software like Excel or Google Sheets. Include categories and subcategories for all your expenses.

Tips for Staying Within Budget

Be Flexible
- Travel Off-Peak: Travel during off-peak seasons to take advantage of lower prices on flights and accommodation.
- Alternative Destinations: Consider less popular destinations that may offer similar experiences at a lower cost.

Save on Accommodation
- Stay Outside City Centers: Accommodations outside city centers can be more affordable.
- Consider Hostels or Vacation Rentals: These options can be cheaper than hotels and offer kitchen facilities for cooking.

Eat Smart
- Local Markets: Buy groceries from local markets and cook some of your meals.
- Street Food: Enjoy affordable and delicious street food options.

Look for Deals
- Discount Passes: Check for city or attraction passes that offer discounts on multiple attractions.
- Free Activities: Research free activities and events at your destination.

Emergency Fund

Set Aside Extra Funds
- Unexpected Expenses: Allocate a portion of your budget for unexpected expenses such as medical emergencies or travel delays.

By planning your budget carefully and using these tips and tools, you can ensure a financially stress-free travel experience. Budgeting allows you to focus on enjoying your trip while staying within your financial means.

FREQUENTLY ASKED QUESTIONS (FAQs)

Why Visit Ohio?

Ohio might not always be the first destination that comes to mind when planning a trip, but it offers a rich tapestry of experiences that can delight every type of traveler. Here's a comprehensive look at why you should visit Ohio, answering some common FAQs.

FAQs About Visiting Ohio

What are the main attractions in Ohio?
- Cedar Point Amusement Park: Known as the "Roller Coaster Capital of the World," it's a must-visit for thrill-seekers.
- Rock and Roll Hall of Fame: Located in Cleveland, this museum celebrates the legends of rock music.
- Hocking Hills State Park: Offers stunning natural beauty with hiking trails, waterfalls, and caves.
- Columbus Zoo and Aquarium: One of the top-rated zoos in the country with a diverse range of exhibits and animals.

Is Ohio family-friendly?
Absolutely! Ohio has numerous attractions perfect for families, including the Columbus Zoo, Kings Island Amusement Park, and the Imagination Station in

Toledo. There are also family-friendly festivals, parks, and interactive museums to explore.

What outdoor activities can you do in Ohio?
- Hiking and Camping: With numerous state parks like Hocking Hills, Mohican State Park, and Cuyahoga Valley National Park, there are plenty of opportunities for hiking, camping, and exploring nature.
- Water Activities: Lake Erie offers boating, fishing, and beach activities. You can also enjoy white-water rafting on the Great Miami River.
- Winter Sports: Snow Trails in Mansfield offers skiing, snowboarding, and tubing.

Is Ohio a good destination for history and culture?
Yes, indeed. Ohio is home to the National Museum of the US Air Force, the Ohio State Reformatory in Mansfield, and various historical sites like the Serpent Mound and Perry's Victory & International Peace Memorial. Cities like Cincinnati and Cleveland also offer rich cultural scenes with museums, theaters, and historic districts.

What's the food scene like in Ohio?
Diverse and Delicious. Ohio's food scene ranges from Amish country cuisine to urban gourmet. Enjoy famous dishes like Cincinnati chili, pierogies in Cleveland, and farm-to-table dining throughout the state. Don't miss

the local breweries and wineries, especially in regions like Geneva-on-the-Lake.

What festivals and events are worth attending?
Plenty to Choose From! Ohio hosts numerous festivals year-round, including the Ohio State Fair, Oktoberfest Zinzinnati, and the Cleveland International Film Festival. Seasonal events like the Fall Harvest Festivals in Amish Country and the Winterfest in Cleveland add to the charm.

Is Ohio affordable for travelers?
Yes. Ohio offers a range of budget-friendly options for accommodations, dining, and activities. Many attractions like state parks and local festivals are either free or reasonably priced, making it an excellent destination for budget-conscious travelers.

Why Visit Ohio?
Ohio provides a unique mix of urban excitement, natural beauty, historical significance, and cultural richness. Whether you're an adventure seeker, history buff, foodie, or family traveler, Ohio has something special to offer. The state's welcoming atmosphere and diverse attractions make it a great destination for a memorable trip.

Getting Current Road Conditions

Staying updated with current road conditions is essential for a safe and smooth journey. Here are some frequently asked questions about how to get real-time road condition updates:

FAQs About Getting Current Road Conditions

How can I find real-time traffic updates?
- Waze: Use the Waze app or visit the (https://www.waze.com/live-map) for real-time traffic updates from other drivers.
- Google Maps: Google Maps provides live traffic information, including accidents, road closures, and construction. You can access it via the Google Maps app or website.

Where can I check road conditions before starting my trip?
- Local Department of Transportation Websites: Many state and local transportation departments have websites with real-time road condition updates.
- The Weather Network: Their highway conditions maps offer radar and satellite images that can help you understand how weather might affect road conditions.

Can I get traffic updates on my phone?
- Traffic Apps: Download apps like Waze, Google Maps, or INRIX Traffic to get real-time traffic updates on your smartphone.
- Text Alerts: Some regions offer text message alerts for road conditions. Check with your local

transportation department to see if this service is available.

How can I stay informed about road conditions while driving?
- Radio Traffic Reports: Tune into local radio stations that provide regular traffic updates.
- Navigation Systems: Use GPS navigation systems or apps that offer live traffic updates and alternative routes.

Are there specific websites for checking road conditions in my area?
- State and Local DOT Websites: Visit the website of your state or local Department of Transportation. They often have dedicated pages for road conditions and traffic updates.
- 511 Services: Many states offer 511 services that provide real-time road condition information via phone, web, and mobile apps.

How do I get updates on road conditions during severe weather?
- Weather Apps: Use weather apps like The Weather Channel or AccuWeather to get updates on severe weather conditions that may affect roads.
- Emergency Alerts: Sign up for emergency alerts from local authorities to receive notifications about road closures and other critical information.

What should I do if I encounter unexpected road conditions?
- Plan Alternative Routes: Use navigation apps to find alternative routes if you encounter unexpected traffic or road closures.
- Stay Informed: Keep an eye on real-time updates through your preferred app or website to stay ahead of any changes in road conditions.

Using these resources and tips can help you stay informed about current road conditions and ensure a safer and more efficient travel experience.

Ohio State Parks Information

Ohio boasts a diverse array of state parks, offering something for everyone, from nature enthusiasts to history buffs. Here are some frequently asked questions about Ohio state parks:

FAQs About Ohio State Parks

How many state parks are there in Ohio?
Ohio has 74 state parks, along with 20 state memorials, 17 state forests, and 12 state wildlife areas.

What activities can I do at Ohio state parks?
Activities vary by park, but you can enjoy hiking, camping, fishing, boating, picnicking, and wildlife

watching. Many parks also offer special events, nature programs, and historical tours.

Are Ohio state parks open year-round?
Yes, most state parks are open year-round and offer a range of seasonal activities. Some parks may have specific hours or seasonal closures, so it's best to check the park's website before visiting.

Do I need a reservation to visit a state park?
Reservations are recommended for camping, cabins, and some popular activities. You can make reservations online through the Ohio State Parks reservation system or by calling the reservation hotline.

Are there any fees to enter Ohio state parks?
Ohio state parks are open and free to the public. However, there may be fees for certain activities, such as camping, cabin rentals, and special events.

What are some of the most popular state parks in Ohio?
Popular parks include Hocking Hills State Park, known for its stunning natural scenery and hiking trails; Cedar Point State Park, home to the famous amusement park; and Caesar Creek State Park, which offers boating, fishing, and camping.

Can I bring my pet to Ohio state parks?
Yes, pets are welcome in many Ohio state parks, but they must be kept on a leash and under control at all times.

Be sure to check the specific park's pet policy before visiting.

What amenities are available at Ohio state parks?
Amenities vary by park, but many offer restrooms, picnic areas, playgrounds, boat ramps, and visitor centers. Some parks also have lodges, cabins, and campgrounds for overnight stays.

How can I find more information about a specific state park?
Visit the Ohio Department of Natural Resources (ODNR) website or the specific park's website for detailed information, maps, and updates on events and closures.

Are there any guided tours or educational programs at Ohio state parks?
Yes, many parks offer guided tours, nature programs, and educational workshops. Check the park's events calendar for upcoming activities and programs.

Ohio state parks provide a wonderful opportunity to explore the natural beauty and rich history of the state. Whether you're looking for a peaceful retreat or an adventurous outing, there's a park for you to enjoy.

Upcoming Fairs and Festivals

Ohio is home to a vibrant calendar of fairs and festivals throughout the year, offering something for everyone. Here are some frequently asked questions about upcoming events:

FAQs About Upcoming Fairs and Festivals

What are some major upcoming fairs and festivals in Ohio?
- Ohio State Fair: Held annually in Columbus, this fair features agricultural exhibits, concerts, rides, and food vendors.
- Cincinnati Music Festival: A large music festival featuring a variety of genres and performances.
- Cleveland International Film Festival: A showcase of independent films from around the world.

Are there any holiday-themed events coming up?
- Holiday Tree Festival: Held in Akron, this festival features beautifully decorated trees and holiday activities.
- PNC Festival of Lights: A popular event in Cincinnati with light displays, holiday music, and activities for families.

What are some craft and holiday markets to look forward to?
- Ohio Made Holiday Market: Located in Columbus, this market features handmade goods from local artisans.
- Holiday Craft Show: Various locations across Ohio host holiday craft shows with unique gifts and decorations.

Are there any food festivals happening soon?
- Oktoberfest Zinzinnati: One of the largest Oktoberfest celebrations in the United States, held in Cincinnati.
- Cincinnati Chili Festival: Celebrates the famous Cincinnati chili with tastings, competitions, and more.

Can I find any outdoor festivals or events?
- Hocking Hills Maple Festival: Held in Hocking Hills, this festival celebrates the maple syrup season with tastings, demonstrations, and activities.
- Caesar Creek Wine and Craft Beer Festival: Offers tastings of local wines and craft beers in a beautiful park setting.

Are there any events for families and children?
- Columbus Zoo's Wildlights: A festive event at the Columbus Zoo with light displays, holiday activities, and animal encounters.

- Butch Bando's Fantasy of Lights: A drive-through light show in Delaware with holiday music and decorations.

How can I find more information about these events?
- OhioFestivals.net: A comprehensive guide to festivals and events in Ohio, with details on dates, locations, and activities.
- Local Tourism Websites: Check the websites of local tourism boards and event organizers for the latest information and updates.

Are there any history?
- Ohio History Connection's Heritage Days: Celebrates Ohio's history with reenactments, demonstrations, and historical exhibits.
- Cleveland Cultural Fest: Showcases the diverse cultures and traditions of the Cleveland area.

Ohio's fairs and festivals offer a wonderful opportunity to experience the state's rich culture, history, and community spirit. Whether you're looking for entertainment, food, crafts, or family fun, there's always something exciting happening.

BONUS SECTION: LOCAL RECIPES TO TRY AT HOME

Ohio Buckeye Candies

Ohio Buckeye Candies are a delightful combination of creamy peanut butter and rich chocolate. While rooted in Ohio tradition, these candies are a crowd favorite at holidays and special gatherings, offering a sweet nod to the state's famous buckeye nut. For the best results, use high-quality chocolate and peanut butter.

Preparation Time
- **Prep**: 15-30 minutes
- **Chilling**: 30 minutes
- **Total**: Approximately 1 hour.

Ingredients
For approximately 60 candies:
- 1 ½ cups creamy peanut butter
- 1 cup unsalted butter (softened)
- ½ teaspoon vanilla extract
- 4 cups powdered sugar (sifted)

Ohio Travel Guide 2025

- 4 cups semisweet chocolate chips
- Toothpicks (for dipping).

Procedure

Prepare the Peanut Butter Mixture
In a mixing bowl, beat the peanut butter, softened butter, and vanilla extract until smooth. Gradually add powdered sugar and continue mixing until fully combined. The mixture should be firm enough to roll into balls.

Form the Balls
Roll the mixture into 1-inch balls and place them on a parchment-lined baking sheet. Insert a toothpick into each ball for easy handling during the dipping process. Freeze the balls for about 30 minutes to harden.

Melt the Chocolate
Melt the chocolate chips in a double boiler or microwave, stirring until smooth.

Dip the Candies
Using the toothpick, dip each frozen ball into the melted chocolate, leaving a small circle of peanut butter visible at the top to resemble the Ohio buckeye nut. Smooth over the toothpick hole if desired.

Set the Candies
Place the dipped balls back on the baking sheet and refrigerate until the chocolate is firm.

Storage
Store the candies in an airtight container in the refrigerator for up to one week, or freeze them for up to three months.

Ohio Travel Guide 2025

Nutritional Value (Per Candy)

- **Calories**: ~150
- **Fat**: ~8-10 g
- Carbohydrates: ~15 g
- Protein: ~2 g
- Sugar: ~13 g

(Note: Values may vary slightly based on ingredient brands and serving size).

Health Benefits

While Buckeye candies are a treat and should be consumed in moderation, they have some nutritional benefits:

- **Peanut Butter**: A source of healthy fats, protein, and essential nutrients like Vitamin E and magnesium.
- **Dark Chocolate (optional)**: Contains antioxidants, which may help reduce inflammation and support heart health.

However, the high sugar content limits their role in a healthy diet.

Portion Recommendation

Given their high sugar and calorie content, limit consumption to 1-2 candies per day as part of a balanced diet. Pairing them with a protein-rich meal or snack can help stabilize blood sugar levels.

Ohio Travel Guide 2025

Cincinnati Chili

Cincinnati chili is a unique regional variation of chili, originating from Cincinnati, Ohio. Unlike traditional chili, it is thinner in consistency and features a distinct blend of Mediterranean-inspired spices, including cinnamon, allspice, and sometimes cloves. Traditionally served over spaghetti and topped with cheese, beans, or onions, Cincinnati chili is both a comfort food and a cultural icon.

Preparation Time
- **Prep Time**: 15 minutes
- **Cook Time**: 2 hours
- **Total Time**: 2 hours 15 minutes

Ingredients
This recipe makes about 6 servings:
- 2 lbs ground beef
- 1 large onion, finely chopped
- 4 cups water or beef broth
- 1 can (15 oz) tomato sauce
- 2 tablespoons chili powder
- 1 teaspoon ground cinnamon

- 1 teaspoon ground allspice
- 1 teaspoon ground cumin
- 1 teaspoon cayenne pepper (adjust for spice preference)
- 1 teaspoon unsweetened cocoa powder
- 2 tablespoons white vinegar
- 1 clove garlic, minced
- Salt to taste

Optional toppings and base

- Cooked spaghetti
- Shredded cheddar cheese
- Diced onions
- Kidney beans
- Oyster crackers

Procedure

Prepare the Base
In a large pot, brown the ground beef over medium heat, breaking it into small pieces. Once browned, drain any excess fat.

Combine Ingredients
Add the chopped onion, garlic, and water (or beef broth) to the pot with the beef. Stir in the tomato sauce, chili powder, cinnamon, allspice, cumin, cayenne pepper, and cocoa powder. Add salt to taste.

Simmer the Chili
Bring the mixture to a boil, then reduce the heat to low. Cover the pot and let it simmer for about 2 hours, stirring occasionally. The chili will thicken slightly, and the flavors will meld together.

Adjust Seasoning
After 2 hours, taste and adjust the seasoning as needed. Add the white vinegar to balance the flavors.

Serve
Cincinnati chili is traditionally served over a plate of cooked spaghetti and topped with shredded cheddar cheese (called a "3-way"). Additional toppings like beans and onions can be added to create a "4-way" or "5-way" variation.

Nutritional Value (Per Serving)

- **Calories**: ~350 (excluding toppings and spaghetti)
- **Protein**: ~20 g
- **Carbohydrates**: ~10 g
- **Fat**: ~20 g
- **Fiber**: ~3 g

Health Benefits

- **Protein-Rich**: Ground beef provides a good source of protein for muscle maintenance and repair.
- **Antioxidants**: Ingredients like cinnamon and cocoa powder are rich in antioxidants, which may help reduce inflammation.
- **Customizable for Dietary Needs**: By using lean ground beef and whole-grain spaghetti or serving it without pasta, Cincinnati chili can be adapted for various dietary preferences.

Portion Recommendation

For a balanced meal, limit portions to 1 cup of chili served over 1 cup of spaghetti. Pair it with a side of fresh vegetables or a small salad for added nutrients.

Cincinnati chili stands out not just for its flavor but also for its versatility, making it a beloved staple in Ohio households and beyond. Whether served at a family gathering or a casual meal, this dish captures the heart of Midwestern cuisine.

APPENDICES

Glossary of Local Terms

When traveling to or within Ohio, you might come across some local terms and phrases unique to the region. Here's a handy glossary of local terms to help you navigate the Buckeye State like a native:

General Terms

Buckeye
- Definition: Refers to both the state tree (the Ohio buckeye) and a nickname for Ohio residents. Also used to describe the Ohio State University sports teams.

O-H-I-O
- Definition: A popular cheer for Ohio State University, often accompanied by forming the letters with one's arms.

The Flats
- Definition: An entertainment district in Cleveland located along the Cuyahoga River, known for its nightlife and dining options.

Three-Way
- Definition: A dish specific to Cincinnati-style chili, consisting of spaghetti topped with chili and a generous amount of shredded cheese.

Ohio Travel Guide 2025

Skyline
- Definition: Refers to Skyline Chili, a famous Cincinnati-based chain known for its unique take on chili.

The Rubber City
- Definition: A nickname for Akron, Ohio, due to its history as a major rubber manufacturing center.

Geographical Terms

The Miami Valley
- Definition: A region in southwestern Ohio that includes the city of Dayton and its surrounding areas.

The Ohio Valley
- Definition: Refers to the Ohio River Valley area, encompassing parts of southeastern Ohio.

The Mahoning Valley
- Definition: A region in northeastern Ohio that includes the cities of Youngstown and Warren.

Local Slang
Pop
- Definition: The regional term for carbonated soft drinks, commonly used in Ohio and other parts of the Midwest.

Sweeper
- Definition: Another term for a vacuum cleaner, used by many Ohioans.

Junction
- Definition: Often used to refer to road intersections, especially in rural areas.

Cultural Terms

Barn Quilt
- Definition: A large, painted quilt pattern displayed on the side of a barn, often found in rural parts of Ohio.

Sauerkraut Balls
- Definition: A popular appetizer in Ohio, particularly in Akron, consisting of sauerkraut mixed with sausage or ham, breaded, and deep-fried.

Goetta
- Definition: A Cincinnati specialty made of ground meat and grains, typically served as a breakfast food.

Festivals and Events

Red, White & Boom!
- Definition: The annual Fourth of July fireworks celebration in Columbus, one of the largest in the Midwest.

ComFest
- Definition: Short for Community Festival, this is a large, free, volunteer-run music and arts festival held annually in Columbus.

Sports Terms

The Horseshoe (The Shoe)
- Definition: The nickname for Ohio Stadium, home of the Ohio State Buckeyes football team.

The Battle of Ohio
- Definition: Refers to the football rivalry game between the Cleveland Browns and the Cincinnati Bengals.

Familiarizing yourself with these local terms can enhance your experience and help you feel more connected to the culture and people of Ohio.

240

Useful Maps and Directions

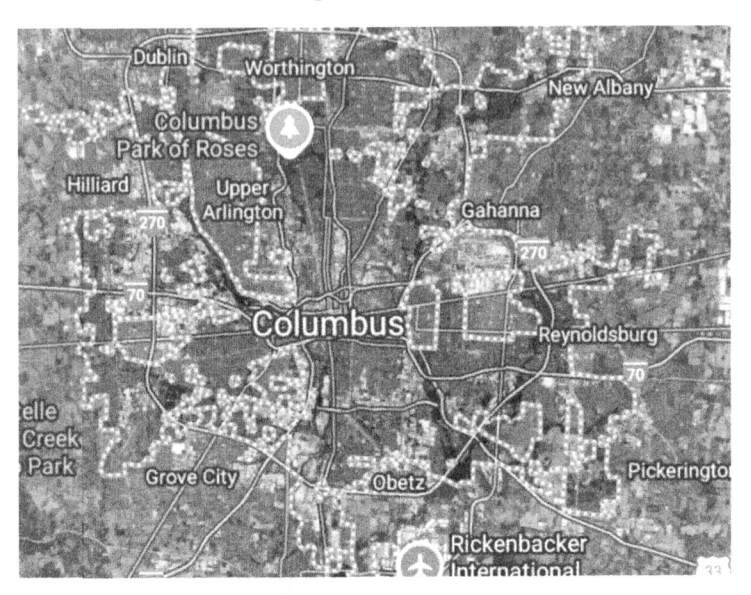

HOW TO SCAN

1. Open your phone's camera.
2. Point it at the QR code.
3. Wait for it to focus.
4. Once recognized, tap the notification.
5. Follow the link or information provided.

COLUMBUS

Ohio Travel Guide 2025

HOW TO SCAN

1. Open your phone's camera.
2. Point it at the QR code.
3. Wait for it to focus.
4. Once recognized, tap the notification.
5. Follow the link or information provided.

CLEVELAND

Ohio Travel Guide 2025

HOW TO SCAN

1. Open your phone's camera.
2. Point it at the QR code.
3. Wait for it to focus.
4. Once recognized, tap the notification.
5. Follow the link or information provided.

TOLEDO

Ohio Travel Guide 2025

243

HOW TO SCAN

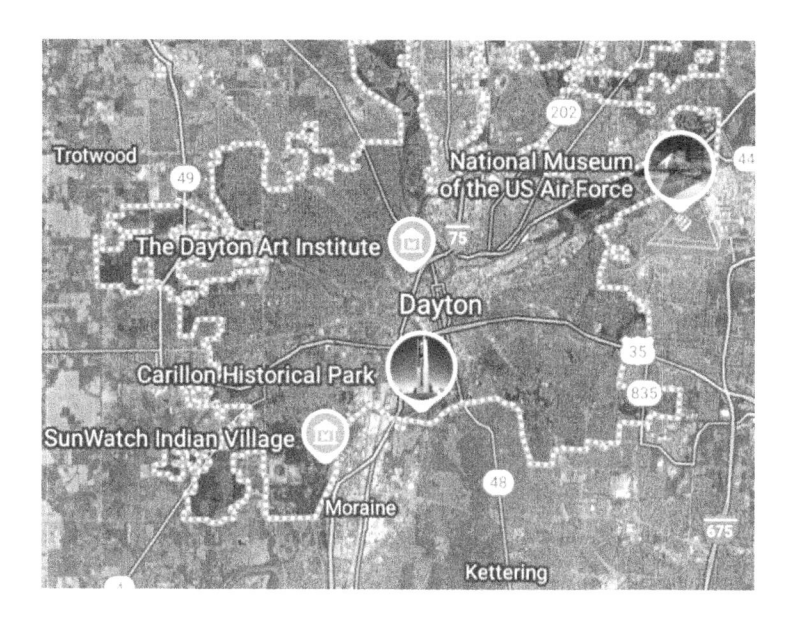

1. Open your phone's camera.
2. Point it at the QR code.
3. Wait for it to focus.
4. Once recognized, tap the notification.
5. Follow the link or information provided.

DAYTON

Ohio Travel Guide 2025

HOW TO SCAN

1. Open your phone's camera.
2. Point it at the QR code.
3. Wait for it to focus.
4. Once recognized, tap the notification.
5. Follow the link or information provided.

CINCINNATI

Ohio Travel Guide 2025

HOW TO SCAN

1. Open your phone's camera.
2. Point it at the QR code.
3. Wait for it to focus.
4. Once recognized, tap the notification.
5. Follow the link or information provided.

Wright Brothers National

Ohio Travel Guide 2025

HOW TO SCAN

1. Open your phone's camera.
2. Point it at the QR code.
3. Wait for it to focus.
4. Once recognized, tap the notification.
5. Follow the link or information provided.

Stan Hywet Hall & Gardens

Ohio Travel Guide 2025

HOW TO SCAN

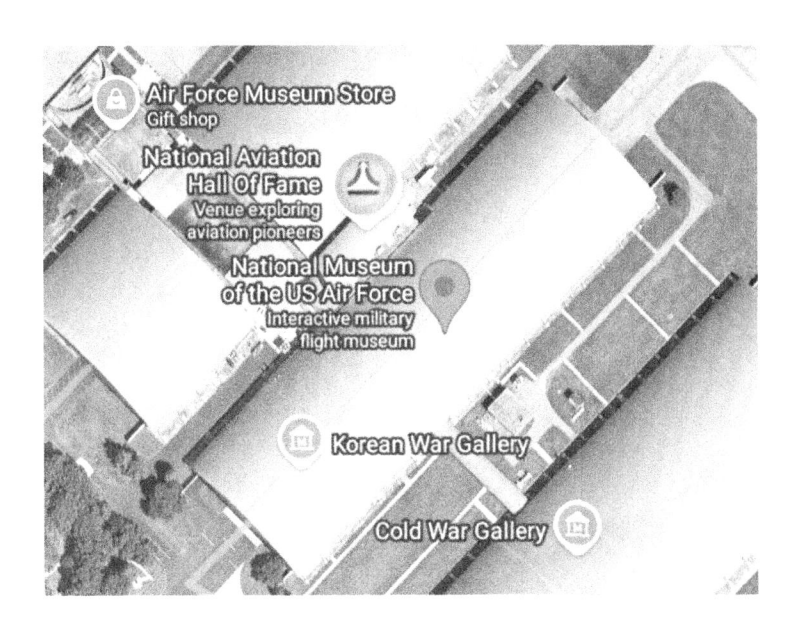

1. Open your phone's camera.
2. Point it at the QR code.
3. Wait for it to focus.
4. Once recognized, tap the notification.
5. Follow the link or information provided.

NATIONAL MUSEUM OF THE US AIR FORCE

Ohio Travel Guide 2025

HOW TO SCAN

1. Open your phone's camera.
2. Point it at the QR code.
3. Wait for it to focus.
4. Once recognized, tap the notification.
5. Follow the link or information provided.

ROCK & ROLL HALL OF FAME

Ohio Travel Guide 2025

249

HOW TO SCAN

1. Open your phone's camera.
2. Point it at the QR code.
3. Wait for it to focus.
4. Once recognized, tap the notification.
5. Follow the link or information provided.

SERPENT MOUND

Ohio Travel Guide 2025

HOW TO SCAN

1. Open your phone's camera.
2. Point it at the QR code.
3. Wait for it to focus.
4. Once recognized, tap the notification.
5. Follow the link or information provided.

OHIO STATE REFORMATORY

Ohio Travel Guide 2025

HOW TO SCAN

1. Open your phone's camera.
2. Point it at the QR code.
3. Wait for it to focus.
4. Once recognized, tap the notification.
5. Follow the link or information provided.

AMISH COUNTRY

Ohio Travel Guide 2025

HOW TO SCAN

1. Open your phone's camera.
2. Point it at the QR code.
3. Wait for it to focus.
4. Once recognized, tap the notification.
5. Follow the link or information provided.

GENEVA-ON-THE-LAKE

Ohio Travel Guide 2025

CONCLUSION

Final Travel Tips

As you embark on your journey, a few final tips can help ensure that your trip is enjoyable, safe, and memorable. Here are some essential travel tips to keep in mind:

Preparation

Research Your Destination
- Local Customs and Etiquette: Understanding the cultural norms and etiquette of your destination can enhance your experience and help you avoid any unintentional faux pas.
- Must-See Attractions: Prioritize the top sights and experiences you don't want to miss.

Pack Wisely
- Essentials: Make a list of essential items such as passports, tickets, chargers, medications, and toiletries.
- Weather-Appropriate Clothing: Check the weather forecast and pack accordingly, including layers for variable climates.

Organize Important Documents
- Copies: Make copies of important documents like your passport, ID, and travel insurance. Store them separately from the originals.

- Digital Backup: Save digital copies of essential documents on a secure cloud service.

During Your Trip

Stay Connected
- Local SIM Cards or Roaming Plans: Consider getting a local SIM card or an international roaming plan to stay connected.
- Wi-Fi: Use Wi-Fi in cafes, hotels, and public areas to save on data costs.

Budget Management
- Track Expenses: Use apps or keep a journal to track your spending and stay within your budget.
- Emergency Funds: Always have a small amount of cash set aside for emergencies.

Health and Safety
- Stay Hydrated: Drink plenty of water, especially if you're in a hot climate or doing physical activities.
- Health Precautions: Follow health guidelines, such as getting necessary vaccinations and bringing pa basic first-aid kit.

Making the Most of Your Experience

Be Open to New Experiences
- Try Local Cuisine: Sample local dishes and drinks to fully experience the culture.

- Engage with Locals: Interacting with residents can provide unique insights and enrich your travel experience.

Capture Memories
- Photography: Take photos of special moments and places, but remember to also enjoy the experience without the lens.
- Travel Journal: Write about your experiences, thoughts, and impressions. It's a great **we** way to reflect on your journey.

Stay Flexible
- Adjust Plans: Be prepared to adjust your plans if necessary. Unexpected changes can lead to new adventures.
- Slow Down: Take time to relax and absorb your surroundings, rather than rushing from one attraction to another.

After Your Trip

Reflect and Share
- Reflect: Take some time to reflect on your experiences, what you learned, and how you've grown.
- Share: Share your stories and photos with friends and family. It can be rewarding to recount your adventures and inspire others.

Traveling is a wonderful opportunity to explore new places, meet new people, and create lasting memories. By staying prepared, open-minded, and flexible, you can make the most of your journey.

Inspirational Quotes

As you prepare to explore the Buckeye State, let these inspirational quotes fuel your journey with excitement, curiosity, and a sense of adventure:

On Adventure and Exploration
- "The world is a book and those who do not travel read only one page." — Saint Augustine
- "Life is either a daring adventure or nothing at all." — Helen Keller
- "Travel far enough, you meet yourself." — David Mitchell

On Discovering New Places
- "Travel makes one modest. You see what a tiny place you occupy in the world." — Gustave Flaubert
- "To travel is to discover that everyone is wrong about other countries." — Aldous Huxley
- "Wherever you go becomes a part of you somehow." — Anita Desai

On Making Memories
- "Collect moments, not things." — Unknown

- "Traveling – it leaves you speechless, then turns you into a storyteller." — Ibn Battuta
- "The journey, not the arrival, matters." — T.S. Eliot

On Embracing the Journey
- "Not all those who wander are lost." — J.R.R. Tolkien
- "We travel not to escape life, but for life not to escape us." — Anonymous
- "Take only memories, leave only footprints." — Chief Seattle

On the Spirit of Adventure
- "Jobs fill your pockets, adventures fill your soul." — Jaime Lyn Beatty
- "Blessed are the curious, for they shall have adventures." — Lovelle Drachman
- "Adventure is worthwhile." — Aesop

On New Experiences
- "The real voyage of discovery consists not in seeking new landscapes, but in having new eyes." — Marcel Proust
- "A journey of a thousand miles begins with a single step." — Lao Tzu
- "Travel is the only thing you buy that makes you richer." — Anonymous

Let these quotes inspire you as you explore Ohio's vibrant cities, stunning landscapes, and rich cultural heritage.

Thank you note

Thank you so much for purchasing the travel guide to Ohio! We are delighted to have you join us on this journey through the Buckeye State.

We hope you find the guide to be a valuable resource, full of insights and tips to enhance your travel experience. Whether you're planning a weekend getaway or an extended adventure, we believe this guide will help you discover the best Ohio has to offer.

Should you have any questions or need further assistance, please do not hesitate to reach out. We're here to ensure you have an amazing time exploring Ohio.

Once again, thank you for your support and trust. We wish you safe travels and unforgettable experiences!

Warm regards,
Sarah H Lokken

Made in the USA
Las Vegas, NV
05 May 2025